QUICK
COLORFUL
QUILTS

QUICK
COLORFUL
QUILTS

edited by

Rosemary Wilkinson

Good Books

Intercourse, PA 17534
800/762-7171
www.goodbks.com

First published in the United States by Good Books.
Intercourse, PA 17534 • 800/762-7171 • www.goodbks.com

Copyright © 2003 New Holland Publishers (UK) Ltd.
All rights reserved.

London • Cape Town • Sydney • Auckland
www.newhollandpublishers.com
Garfield House, 86-88 Edgeware Road, London W2 2EA
80 McKenzie Street, Cape Town 8091, South Africa
Unit 4, 14 Aquatic Drive, Frenchs Forest, NSW 2086, Australia
218 Lake Road, Northcote, Auckland, New Zealand

Text, photography, and illustrations © 2003 New Holland Publishers (UK) Ltd.
Quilt designs copyright © Frances de Rees, Katharine Guerrier, Clair Higgott, Jean Hunt, Gill Turley,
Rose Verney, Sarah Wellfair, Rosemary Wilkinson, Margaret Wise, Dorothy Wood
Copyright © 2003 New Holland Publishers (UK) Ltd

Editor: Rosemary Wilkinson
Design: Frances de Rees
Photography: Shona Wood
Illustraitons: Carrie Hill
Template diagrams: Kuo Kang Chen

Reproduction by Pica Digital PTE Ltd, Singapore
Printed and bound in China

ACKNOWLEDGMENTS
The Publishers would like to thank Rowan fabrics for supplying the shot cotton fabrics for "Apricot Wave."
Thanks also to Rita Whitehorn for making up and checking the pattern for "Flower Strippy."

NOTE
The measurements for each project are given in imperial and metric.
Use only one set of measurements — do not interchange them because they are not direct equivalents.

QUICK COLORFUL QUILTS
Good Books, Intercourse, PA 17534
International Standard Book Number: 1-56148-372-9
Library of Congress Catalog Card Number: 2003049065

Library of Congress Cataloging-in-Publication Data
Quick colorful quilts : 15 sizzling new fast and easy quilts / edited by Rosemary Wilkinson.
p. cm.
ISBN 1-56148-372-9
1. Patchwork--Patterns. 2. Quilting--Patterns. I. Wilkinson, Rosemary.
TT835.Q4535 2003
746.46'041--dc21   2003049065

CONTENTS

Basic Quick Techniques

Although there is evidence that pieced or patchwork quilts were used as early as the 1600s, the craft is probably most frequently associated with the pioneering settlers making a new life in America. Of necessity they used every scrap of fabric available to make quilts to keep their families warm in the harsh winters. It is probable that the pieced "blocks" so associated with American patchwork were first created to enable them to stitch while making the long journeys to find a new home. During the bicentennial celebrations of the American Independence there was a great resurgence in the craft, which in turn spawned the enormous worldwide quilting industry of today.

This industry and the quilters who feed it have created the many and varied tools which make the craft so much easier and faster today. These tools not only enable patchwork to be assembled with the speed that the world finds so essential now, but they also produce a greater accuracy in the cutting and piecing of the individual components that make up a patchwork quilt. The quilts in this book all make use of these tools and techniques.

FABRICS

Fabric selection is always a personal choice. For each of the quilts in this book we have photographed swatches of the fabrics used to aid in identification. However, you don't need to use the same colors, and there are four alternative colorways with each design to suggest other possibilities which might suit your purpose better.

To make a successful quilt, there needs to be a difference in tonal values - fabrics that read as light, medium or dark. A selection of fabrics can be all "light" or "dark" but among them there should be a difference in value - depth of color. To help in seeing these values when choosing your fabrics, squint your eyes, look through a camera, or the wrong end of binoculars. A variation in the scale of a printed design can also add interest to a quilt. The addition of plain fabrics or those that read plain, such as tone-on-tone prints, can also enhance the overall appearance.

QUANTITIES

The quantities given at the beginning of each project have been calculated to allow for a bit extra - just in case! The various pieces/strips cut for each quilt use the rotary cutting method and, unless otherwise stated, are cut

from across the width of the fabric. Templates are sometimes used to cut shapes. If these are not given as full size, enlarge them on a photocopier.

A few of the quilts combine cutting on the length of the fabric with cutting across the width. This is to make the most economical use of fabric or to obtain border pieces cut in one piece.

Unless otherwise stated, any ¼ yard/ 25 cm requirement is the "long" quarter – the full width of the fabric – and not the "fat" quarter which is a piece 18 x 22 in/50 x 56 cm.

TYPES

100% cotton is probably the easiest to handle; it doesn't fray too readily and is easily finger-creased, but fabric types are very much a personal preference and are, of course, chosen for specific projects. Bed quilts are usually made using 100% cottons but for wallhangings or "art quilts" – anything goes.

PREPARATION

All fabrics should be washed prior to use in order to wash out any excess dye and to avoid fabrics shrinking at different rates. Wash each fabric separately and rinse - repeatedly if necessary - until the water is clear of any color run. If washing in a machine, cut a piece of white fabric from a

larger piece. Place one piece in with the wash. After the wash, compare the white fabric with its other half. If they are the same, the fabric did not run. If a particular fabric continues to color the water no matter how many times it is washed/rinsed and you have your heart set on using it, try washing it together with a small piece of each of the fabrics you intend to use with it. If these fabrics retain their original color, i.e. they match the pieces not washed with the offending fabric, you would probably be safe in using it. But if in doubt - don't! Abandon it and choose another.

Once washed and before they are completely dry, iron the fabrics and fold them selvage to selvage - as they were originally on the bolt - in preparation for cutting. Be sure to fold them straight so that the selvages line up evenly, even if the cut edges are not parallel (this will be fixed later).

THREADS

For machine quilting, lightweight or monofilament threads are usual. For quilting by hand, use a thread labeled "quilting thread" which is heavier than normal sewing thread. There are several manufacturers of this thread and it comes in many different colors. Some threads are 100% cotton; others have a polyester core that is wrapped with cotton. You can use a thread either to match or to contrast with the fabric that is being quilted. It is also acceptable to use several colors on the same piece of work. If the quilt is to be tied rather than quilted, a heavier thread, such as coton perlé or coton à broder is used.

HOOPS AND FRAMES

The quilt should be held in a hoop or frame for consistency of tension while hand quilting. There are many types available ranging from hoops, round and oval, to standing frames made of plastic pipes to wooden fixed frames that are in themselves magnificent pieces of furniture.

Hoops are perhaps the easiest for a beginner to start using. The 14 in/ 35 cm or 16 in/40 cm are best for portability. Many quilters continue to use hoops in preference to standing frames. As with any equipment, it all comes down to personal preferences. When the quilt is in the hoop, the surface of the quilt should not be taut, as is the case with embroidery. If you place the quilt top with its hoop on a table you should be able to push the fabric in the center of the hoop with your finger and touch the table beneath. Without this "give" you will not be able to "rock" the needle for the quilting stitch. Whatever you use, never leave the quilt fastened in a hoop. Get into the practice of releasing the outside hoop whenever you leave the quilt – even if only for a few minutes. Those few minutes could develop into several days!

EQUIPMENT

The tools of the trade for the modern quilter make life much easier than for those who stitched patchwork in the past. If you are new to patchwork and quilting, the tools available today can be expensive but are well worth the money for the accuracy and speed they afford the user.

Scissors: These are obviously a necessity. Two pairs are recommended. One pair of good quality scissors should be used for cutting fabric and only fabric. The second pair is for cutting paper, card, or template plastic.

Pencils: These will occasionally be required. They need to be sharp at all times to maintain accuracy. The modern "use and throw away" propelling pencils are ideal for this purpose both for drawing around templates and for use in marking quilting designs on quilt tops.

Markers: Quilting designs can either be traced or drawn on the fabric prior to the layering or added after the layering with the aid of stencils or templates. Various marking tools are available: 2H pencils, silver, yellow, white pencils; fade away or washable marking pens. Whatever your choice, test the markers on a scrap of the fabric used in the quilt to ensure that the marks are indeed removable.

Pins: Good quality, clean, rustproof, straight pins are essential when a pin is required to hold the work in place for piecing. Flat-headed flower pins are useful because they don't add bulk.

Safety pins: More quilters are now using safety pins to hold the quilt "sandwich" together for quilting, especially those who prefer to machine quilt or want the speed of not tacking/basting the three layers together.

Needles: For hand quilting use "quilting" or "betweens" needles. Most quilters start with a no. 8 or 9 and progress to a no. 10 or no. 12. The larger the number, the smaller the needle. For machine stitching, the needles numbered 70/10 or 80/12 are both suitable for piecing and quilting. Some makers have needles that are labeled "quilting."

Thimbles: Two thimbles will be required for quilting. One thimble is worn on the hand pushing the needle and the other on the hand underneath the quilt "receiving" the needle. There are many and varied types on the market ranging from the usual metal thimbles to those made of plastic to leather sheaths for the finger. There are also little patches that stick to the finger to protect it from the needle pricks. Whatever method is your choice, it is strongly advised that you do use some protection for the fingers on both hands.

ROTARY CUTTING

Rotary cutting has become the most commonly used method to cut fabrics for patchwork today. Special cutters,

rulers, and mats are needed, and with this equipment quilts can be made more accurately and assembled quickly.

ROTARY CUTTERS
There are several different makes available, mainly in three different sizes: small, medium, and large. The medium size (45mm) is probably the one most widely used and perhaps the easiest to control. The smallest can be difficult to use with rulers. The largest is very useful when cutting many layers of fabric but can take some practice to use.

RULERS
There are many different rulers available for use with rotary cutters. These are made of acrylic and are sufficiently thick to act as a guide for the rotary blade. You must use these rulers with the rotary cutter. Do not use metal rulers, as they will severely damage the blades.

Ideally the rulers should have the markings on the underside, laser printed and easy to read. Angle lines are also useful and should be marked in both directions. Different makes of rulers can have the lines printed in different colors. Choose one that you find easy on your eyes. Some makes also have a non-slip surface on the back – a very helpful addition.

To start, the two most useful basic rulers are either a 24 x 6 in/60 x 15 cm or one that is slightly shorter and the small bias square ruler, 6½ in or 15 cm. This ruler is particularly useful for marking squares containing two triangles – the half-square triangle units. There are many other rulers designed for specific jobs that you can purchase if and when needed.

SELF-HEALING ROTARY CUTTING MATS
These are an essential companion to the rotary cutter and ruler. Do not attempt to cut on any other surface. The mats come in a number of different sizes and several different colors. The smaller ones are useful to take to classes or workshops, but for use at home, purchase the largest that you feel you can afford and that suits your own workstation. There is usually a grid on one side. The lines on the mat

are not always accurate, so get into the habit of using the lines on the ruler rather than the ones on the mat. Most rotary cutting tools are available with either imperial or metric measurements.

MEASUREMENTS
The measurements in the quilt instructions are given in both imperial and metric. Use only one set of measurements in any project – do not interchange them because they are not direct equivalents.

SEAMS
Unless otherwise stated, the seam allowances which will be included in the measurements given are ¼ in for imperial and 0.75 cm for metric. The metric seam allowance is slightly bigger than the imperial, but it is easy to use in conjunction with the various rotary cutting rulers on the market.

If you wish to adapt any of the projects, remember the following when making your calculations:
Imperial: Add the following to the finished size measurements:
Seam allowance: ¼ in
Cutting strips/squares/rectangles: add ½ in
Cutting half-square triangles: add ⅞ in
Cutting quarter-square triangles: add 1¼ in
Metric: Add the following to the finished size measurements:
Seam allowance: 0.75 cm
Cutting strips/squares/rectangles: add 1.5 cm

Cutting half-square triangles: add 2.5 cm
Cutting quarter-square triangles: add 3.5 cm
See diagrams 1 and 2 to see how the measurements for half- and quarter-square triangles are calculated.

diagram 1

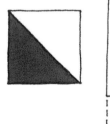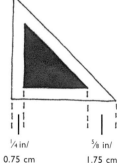

¼ in/
0.75 cm

⅝ in/
1.75 cm

diagram 2

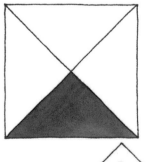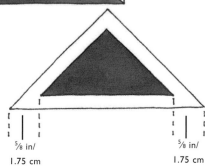

⅝ in/
1.75 cm

⅝ in/
1.75 cm

MAKING THE EDGE STRAIGHT

1 The cut edge of the fabric will probably not be straight, so place the prepared fabric – folded selvage to selvage – on the cutting mat with the bulk of the fabric on the side that is not your cutting hand. Place the ruler on the fabric towards the cut edge, aligning the horizontal lines on the ruler with the fold of the fabric and with the selvage.

2 Place your fingers on the ruler to hold it straight and apply pressure. Keep the hand holding the ruler in line with the hand cutting the fabric. Place the cutter on the mat just off the fabric and up against the ruler. Start cutting by running the cutter alongside and right up next to the edge of the ruler (diagram 3).

diagram 3

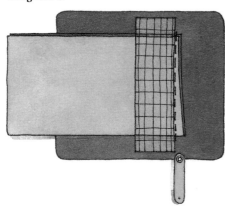

3 When the cutter becomes level with your extended fingertips, stop cutting, but leave the cutter in position and carefully move the hand holding the ruler further along the ruler to keep the applied pressure in the area where the cutting is taking place. Continue cutting and moving the steadying hand as necessary until you have cut completely across the fabric. As soon as the cut is complete, close the safety shield on the cutter.

4 Open out the narrow strip of fabric just cut off. Check to make sure that a "valley" or a "hill" has not appeared at the point of the fold; it should be perfectly straight. If it is not, the fabric was not folded correctly. Fold the fabric again, making sure that this time the selvages are exactly aligned. Make another cut to straighten the end and check again.

CUTTING STRIPS

1 Once the end is straight, put the fabric on the cutting mat on the side of your cutting hand. Place the ruler on the mat so that it overlaps the fabric. The cut edge of the fabric should be aligned with the vertical line on the ruler that corresponds to the measurement that you wish to cut, and the horizontal lines on the ruler should be aligned with the folded edge and the selvage of the fabric.

2 As before, place one hand on the ruler to apply pressure while cutting the fabric with the other hand (diagram 4).

diagram 4

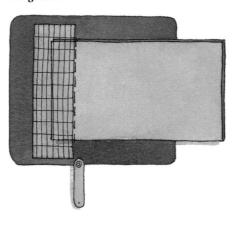

CROSS-CUTTING
Squares

1 First cut a strip to the measurement required.

2 Place the strip just cut on the cutting mat with the longest edge horizontal to you. Straighten off one end as before.

3 Now cut across (cross-cut) the strip, using the same measurement used when cutting the strip and ensuring that the horizontal lines of the ruler

diagram 5

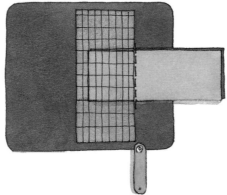

It is wise when cutting a number of strips – say for a log cabin quilt – to open out a strip occasionally and check that it is still straight at the point of the fold. A slight error on one or two strips is not a disaster, but the more strips you cut, the greater the error, and you can end up with strips that cannot be used.

align with the horizontal edge of the fabric. You have now created squares of the required measurement (diagram 5).

Rectangles

1 First cut a strip to one of the required side measurements for the rectangle.

2 Turn the strip to the horizontal position as for the squares.

3 Cross-cut this strip using the other side measurement required for the rectangle. Again, ensure that the horizontal lines of the ruler align with the horizontal cut edges of the strip.

Wide Strips

Placing two rulers side by side can aid the cutting of extra wide strips. If you don't have two rulers, place the fabric on the cutting mat in the correct position for cutting. Align the cut edge of the fabric with one of the vertical lines running completely across the cutting board and the folded edge with one of the horizontal lines on the mat. If the measurement does not fall on one of the lines on the cutting mat, use the ruler in conjunction with the cutting mat.

Half-Square Triangles

1 Cut a strip to the measurement required.

2 Cross-cut the strip into squares using the same cut measurement.

3 Align the 45° angle line on the ruler with the sides of the square and place the edge of the ruler so that it goes diagonally across the square from corner to corner. Cut the square on

diagram 6

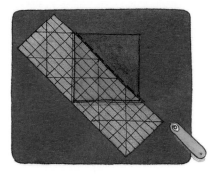

this diagonal creating two half-square triangles (diagram 6).

Quarter-Square Triangles

1 Cut the fabric into strips of the correct depth.

2 Cut the strips into squares of the correct width.

3 Align the edge of the ruler with diagonally opposite corners and the 45° line with the side of the square, then cut across the diagonal.

4 You can either repeat this procedure on the other diagonal, or if you are wary of the fabric slipping now that it is in two pieces, separate the two triangles and cut them individually. Align one of the horizontal lines of the ruler with the long edge of the triangle, the 45° line with the short edge of the triangle, and the edge of the ruler placed on the point of the triangle opposite the long edge. Cut this half-square triangle into two quarter-square triangles. Repeat with the remaining half-square triangle (diagram 7).

diagram 7

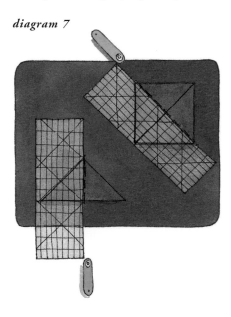

Multi-Strip Units

Cut the required number and size of strips and stitch together as per the instructions for the block/quilt you are making. Press the seams and check that they are pressed flat on the right side of the strip unit with no pleats or folds.

Place the unit right side up in the horizontal position on the cutting mat. This time when cutting to the required measurement there are more reference points to ensure that you are cutting straight. Align the horizontal lines on the ruler with the cut edges of the strips and with the seam lines just created. If after cutting a few cross-cuts the lines on the ruler do not line up with the cut edges as well as the seam lines, re-cut the end to straighten it before cutting any more units (diagram 8).

diagram 8

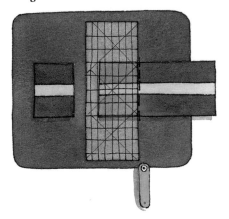

MACHINE STITCHING

As previously mentioned, the seam allowances used in this book are the imperial ¼ in or the metric 0.75 cm. To stitch accurately, you must be able to use the correct seam allowance and know where this is on your own machine. Many machines today have a "¼ in" or "patchwork" foot available as an extra. There are also various generic foot accessories available which will fit most machines. Don't assume that the foot on your machine is of the correct width. Check first, as follows:

Unthread the machine. Place a piece of paper under the presser foot, so that the righthand edge of the paper aligns with the righthand edge of the presser foot. Stitch a seam line on the paper. A row of holes will appear.

Remove the paper from the machine and measure the distance from the holes to the edge of the paper. If it is not the correct width, try one of the following methods.

1 If your machine has a number of different needle positions, try moving the needle in the direction required to make the seam allowance accurate. Try the test of stitching a row of holes again. If this does not work, there is another way.

2 Draw a line on the paper to the correct seam allowance, i.e. ¼ in/0.75 cm from the edge of the paper. Place the paper under the presser foot, aligning the drawn line with the needle. Lower the presser foot to hold the paper securely, and to double check, lower the needle to ensure that it is directly on top of the drawn line.

Now put some masking tape on the bed of the machine so that the lefthand edge of the tape lines up with the righthand edge of the paper. This can also be done with magnetic strips available on the market to be used as seam guides. But do take advice on using these if your machine is computerized or electronic.

When stitching pieces together, line the edge of the fabric up with the righthand edge of the presser foot. Assuming that the foot is of the correct width, or that you have moved the needle into a position to create the correct width, this will give you an accurate seam allowance. If you have used tape or the magnetic strip on the bed of your machine, line the righthand edge of the fabric up with the lefthand edge of the tape to give you an accurate seam allowance.

To double check you have the correct seam allowance, cut three strips of fabric 1½ in/4 cm wide. Stitch these together. Press the seams away from the center strip. Measure the center strip. It should measure exactly 1 in/2.5 cm wide. If not, reposition the needle/tape and try again.

The stitch length used is normally 12 stitches to the inch or 5 stitches to the centimeter. If the pieces being stitched together are to be cross-cut into smaller units, it is probably advisable to slightly shorten the stitch. It is also good practice to start each new

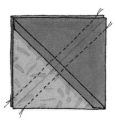
project with a new needle in a clean machine – free of fluff around the bobbin housing.

QUICK PIECING
Chain Piecing
Chain piecing is a process much used in quick pieced projects. Place the first two pieces or strips in the machine, right sides together, and stitch them together. Just before reaching the end stop stitching and pick up the next two pieces or strips. Place them on the bed of the machine so that they just touch the pieces under the needle. Stitch off one set and onto the next. Repeat this process until all the pairs are stitched. You have created a "chain" of pieced patches/strips (diagram 9). Cut the thread between each unit to separate them. Press the seams according to the instructions given with each project.

diagram 9

Tip:

To further speed up this process, place the two pieces/strips to be stitched together beside the sewing machine. Place one group of patches facing up and one group facing down. Now when you pick up one piece, its partner is in the correct position to place on top, right sides together.

PRESSING
Each individual project will have instructions on the direction in which to press the seam allowances. These have been designed to facilitate easier piecing at junctions and to reduce the bulk so that seam allowances do not

lay one on top of the other. Pressing as you complete each stage of the piecing will also improve the accuracy and look of your work. Take care not to distort the patches. Be gentle, not fierce, with the iron.

Two-Triangle or Bi-Colored Squares
1 Cut two squares of different colored fabrics to the correct measurement, i.e. the finished size of the square containing the two triangles + ⅞ in/ 2.5 cm. Place them right sides together aligning all raw edges. On the wrong side of one of the squares draw a line diagonally from one corner to the other.
2 Stitch ¼ in/0.75 cm on either side of the drawn line.
3 Cut the two halves apart by cutting on the drawn line. You now have two squares each containing two triangles. Press the seams towards the darker of the two fabrics (diagram 10).

diagram 10

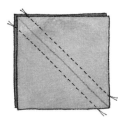

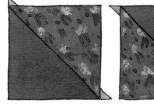

Four-Triangle Squares
1 Cut squares to the finished size of the square containing four triangles + 1¼ in/3.5 cm. Follow the stitching, cutting apart, and pressing sequence as for two triangles in a square.
2 Place the two squares containing the two triangles right sides together. Ensure that each triangle is not facing a triangle of the same color. Draw a line diagonally from corner to corner, at right angles to the previously stitched seam.
3 Stitch ¼ in/0.75 cm on either side of this drawn line. Before cutting apart, open up each side and check to see that the points match in the center. Cut apart on the drawn line.

You now have two squares each containing four triangles (diagram 11).

diagram 11

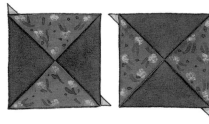

ADDING BORDERS
Abutted Corners
This treatment of the corners on borders for quilts is perhaps the easiest and requires less fabric. The measurements for the borders required for each quilt in the book will be given in the instructions. It is, however, always wise to measure your own work to determine the actual measurement.
1 Measure the quilt through the center across the width edge to edge. Cut the strips for the top and bottom borders to this length by the width required for the border.
2 Pin the strips to the quilt by pinning first at each end, then in the middle, then evenly spaced along the edge. By pinning in this manner it is possible to ensure that the quilt "fits" the border. Stitch the border strips into position on the top and bottom edge of the quilt (diagram 12). Press the seams towards the border.

diagram 12

3 Measure the quilt through the center top to bottom. Cut the side border strips to this measurement.
4 Pin and stitch the borders to each side of the quilt as before

(diagram 13). Press the seams towards the border.

diagram 13

Mitered Corners

This treatment requires a bit more effort but often gives the quilt a more professional finish.

1 Measure the quilt through the center in both directions to give the starting measurements for the borders.
2 To these measurements add twice the width of the border, then add seam allowances of about 2 in/5 cm. Cut strips to the correct measurement for the top, bottom, and sides.
3 On the wrong side of the border fabric, place your rotary cutting ruler with a 45° line on it aligning with one of the long edges of the border. Position the ruler towards one end of the border strip, leaving sufficient seam allowance between the edge of the ruler and the end of the strip, and draw a line along the edge of the ruler. This will be the mitered corner stitching line (diagram 14).

diagram 14

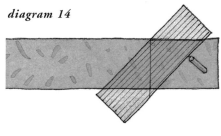

4 Measure ¼ in/0.75 cm up from the edge of the border and make a mark at the point where it crosses the 45° drawn line (diagram 15).

diagram 15

5 From the mark just made measure the length of that border piece – side or top/bottom finished quilt measure-

ment – and make a mark ¼ in/0.75 cm up from the long edge.
6 Align the ruler with the mark just made, with the ruler pointing out towards the nearest end of the border strip, and aligning the 45° line on the ruler with the edge of the border strip. Draw a line – the stitching line for the mitered corner (diagram 16).

diagram 16

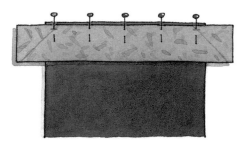

7 Repeat steps 3 to 6 for all four border strips.
8 Place a border strip along the appropriate edge of the quilt. Stick a pin through the mark made ¼ in/0.75 cm from the edge of the border to a corresponding mark made on the quilt top ¼ in/0.75 cm from each edge. Pin both ends, the middle, and evenly along the edge (diagram 17).

diagram 17

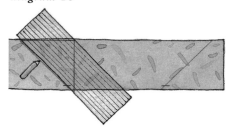

9 Start stitching the border to the quilt at the mark, securing with backstitching, and continue to the mark at the other end, also securing by backstitching. Open out and press the seam. Stitch on all four borders in this manner.
10 Fold the quilt diagonally, so that two adjacent border strips are right sides together. Align the drawn miter lines by sticking pins in on the line on the border piece laying on top and ensuring that the pin comes out on the line on the border piece underneath (diagram 18).

diagram 18

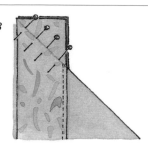

11 Stitch the two border pieces together along the drawn line and up to the point where they meet the quilt. Secure by backstitching. Open out the border and check that the seam just stitched is correct. Trim the excess fabric to the ¼ in/0.75 cm seam allowance. Press the seam open.

QUILTING

The three layers or "sandwich" of the backing/wadding/quilt top are ultimately held together by the quilting. The quilting can either be done by hand or machine.

Layering/Sandwiching

Prior to any quilting, unless you are using a longarm quilting machine (see page 14), the pieced top must be layered with the wadding and the backing. The wadding and the backing should be slightly larger than the quilt top – approximately 2 in/5 cm on all sides.

1 Lay out the backing fabric wrong side uppermost. Ensure that it is stretched out and smooth. Securing the edges with masking tape placed at intervals along the edges can help to hold it in position.
2 Place the wadding on top of the backing fabric. If you need to join two pieces of wadding first, do so by butting the edges and stitching together by hand using a herringbone stitch (diagram 19).

diagram 19

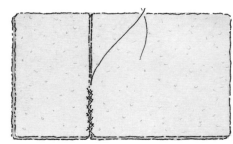

3 Place the pieced top right side up and centered on top of the wadding.

Basting

The three layers now need to be held together for quilting. This can be done by basting by hand or by the use of safety pins. For either method, start in the center of the quilt and work out to the edges.

Using a long length of thread start basting in the center of the quilt top. Only pull about half of the thread through as you start stitching. Once you have reached the edge, go back and thread the other end of the thread and baste to the opposite edge. Repeat this process, stitching in a grid over the whole quilt top (diagram 20).

diagram 20

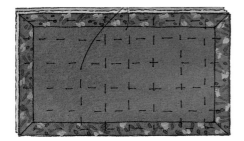

Machine Quilting

In this form of quilting a continuous line of stitching will be visible both on the top and on the back of the quilt. Many consider machine quilting to be the quicker option. If the quilting is mainly functional and not highly decorative, perhaps this is true. However, to machine quilt well – as with any discipline – takes practice.

Before commencing work on the quilt, make up a practice sandwich – if possible using the same fabrics and wadding as used in the actual quilt. Using the threads that you intend to use on the quilt, have a practice session to determine the effect you want. Some machines require a walking foot

NOTE For easier handling, roll a large quilt "scroll" fashion to fit within the machine space.

Tip:

If basting for machine quilting, keep the stitches on the top short so they do not so easily catch on the foot of the sewing machine.

If using safety pins, these should also be placed at intervals over the quilt, forming a grid, with each pin being no further apart than the width of your hand. The pins used should be fine and rustproof like the ones dry cleaners use.

to stitch the three layers together. These are used with the feed dogs up, and, while in use, the machine controls the direction and stitch length. This can restrict you to only straight line quilting, such as "in the ditch" (stitching just beside a seam line on the side without the seam allowances) or very gentle curves. Tight curves and any freehand quilting will be done using a darning foot with the feed dogs down.

When starting and stopping the stitching during machine quilting, either reduce the stitch length to zero or stitch several stitches in one spot. If you do not like the build up of stitches that this method produces, leave long tails on the thread when you start and stop. Later pull these threads through to one side of the quilt, knot them, then thread them into a needle. Push the needle into the fabric and into the wadding, but not through to the other side of the quilt, and then back out through the fabric, again about 1 in/2.5 cm away from where the needle entered the quilt. Cut off the excess thread.

Free Motion Machine Quilting

When machine quilting in a freehand manner, a darning foot is used with the feed dogs down. With this machine set-up, you can move the quilt forwards, backwards and sideways. Some machines are happier than others doing this, but it takes hours of practice to do it well. Designs to be used for machine quilting should ideally be those that have one continuous line. If using a free form squiggle as a background, be sure to keep the

density of stitching the same. Don't get over-enthusiastic when you start a project and make the stitching designs close together, only to tire of the process later and begin to space them out.

There are many and varied tools on the market which are designed to help make handling the quilt easier during the machine quilting process. But the most essential tool is practice.

Hand Quilting

The stitch used for hand quilting is a running stitch. The needle goes into the quilt through to the back and returns to the top of the quilt all in one movement. The aim is to have even stitches. Size of stitches and spaces between the stitches should ideally all be the same.

1 Thread a needle with an 18 in/45 cm length of quilting thread and knot the end. Push the needle into the fabric and into the wadding, but not through to the back, about 1 in/2.5 cm away from where you want to start stitching. Bring the needle up through the fabric at the point where you will begin stitching. Gently pull on the thread to "pop" the knot through and into the wadding.

2 To make a perfect quilting stitch, the needle needs to enter the fabric perpendicular to the quilt top. Holding the needle between your first finger and thumb, push the needle into the fabric until it hits the thimble on the finger of the hand underneath.

3 The needle can now be held between the thimble on your sewing hand and the thimble on the finger underneath. Release your thumb and first finger hold on the needle. Place your thumb on the quilt top, just in front of the position where the needle will come back up to the top, and gently press down on the quilt top (diagram 21).

diagram 21

4 At the same time, rock the thread end of the needle back down towards the quilt top and push the needle up from underneath so that the point appears on the top of the quilt. You can either pull the needle through, now making only one stitch, or rock the needle up to the vertical again, push the needle into the quilt top, then rock the needle back down to the quilt top, again placing another stitch on the needle. Repeat until you can no longer rock the needle into a completely upright position. Pull the needle through the quilt (diagram 22).

diagram 22

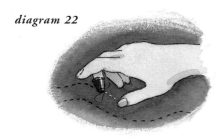

5 One stitch at a time or several placed on the needle at once – "the rocking stitch" – before pulling the thread through, are both acceptable. When the stitching is complete, tie a knot in the thread close to the quilt surface. Push the needle into the quilt top and the wadding but not through to the back of the quilt. Bring the needle up again, about 1 in/2.5 cm away, and gently tug on the thread to "pop" the knot through the fabric and into the wadding. Cut the thread.

Big Stitch Quilting

There is another form of hand quilting popular today, known as the "Big Stitch," which can speed up the process of quilting by hand and adds yet another design element. Big Stitch uses coton perlé no. 8 as the thread and obviously a larger needle with a bigger eye. The stitches are also larger, and simplicity is required for the quilting designs used. It can be very effective but is not necessarily suited to all quilts. Apart from simple designs, any outline quilting is normally ½ in/1.25 cm from the seam lines rather than the ¼ in/0.75 cm used with traditional hand quilting. The quilting stitch for the "Big Stitch" is also a running stitch.

LONGARM QUILTING MACHINES

Since the advent of longarm quilting machines it is possible to have quilts professionally quilted. You can choose from a huge library of quilting designs. There is also the option to have edge-to-edge quilting; all-over quilting of one design over the entire quilt, or a combination of patterns to complement each other, e.g. medallions, feathers, cables, and cross-hatching. Alternatively, you can specify your own freehand style.

The pieced top, wadding, and backing are mounted onto separate rollers which are part of the frame of the machine. This means that the three layers of the quilt need not be tacked together in the conventional way.

The machine is hand operated and takes considerable skill to operate successfully. Most of the quilters who offer these services advertise in patchwork magazines and will provide you with an explanatory brochure.

BINDING

Once the quilting is completed, the quilt is usually finished with a binding to enclose the raw edges. This binding can be cut on the straight or on the bias. Either way, the binding is usually best done with a double fold. If cut straight, cut the strips, then join them together to form one continuous strip. If bias cut, join the strips with a diagonal seam (diagram 23).

diagram 23

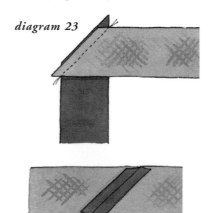

To make continuous bias binding:
1 Cut a square of fabric and mark the edges, A, B, C, and D. Cut in half by cutting on the diagonal. With right sides together, place side A on top of side B and stitch together taking the usual

¼ in/0.75 cm seam allowance (diagram 24).

diagram 24

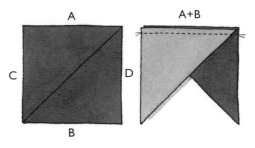

2 Open out the unit and press the seam open. On the wrong side draw lines to mark the width of the bias strips you require (diagram 25).

diagram 25

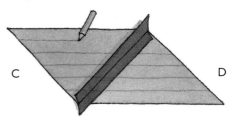

3 With right sides together, join side C to side D, but instead of matching the drawn lines, offset them by one row. Pin the edges to ensure that the lines match. Stitch, then press the seam open.
4 Now, using scissors, cut a continuous strip along the drawn line, following it around the tube you have just created (diagram 26).

diagram 26

Double-Fold Binding

The width of the bias strips should be cut to the following measurement: finished binding width x four + the seam allowance x two. Example:
A finished binding width of ½ in would be cut as 2½ in: (½ in x 4) + (¼ in x 2) = 2½ in
or 1.25 cm would be cut 6.5 cm: (1.25 cm x 4) + (0.75 cm x 2) = 6.5 cm

1 Fold the binding in half lengthwise with wrong sides together and lightly press.

2 Place the binding's raw edges to the raw edge of the quilt – somewhere along one side; not at a corner. Commence stitching about 1 in/2.5 cm from the end of the binding, and using ¼ in/0.75 cm seam allowance, stitch the binding to the quilt through all layers of the "sandwich," stopping ¼ in/0.75 cm from the end. At this point, backstitch to secure, then break off the threads. Remove the quilt from the sewing machine.

3 Place the quilt on a flat surface with the binding just stitched at the top edge and fold the binding strip up and away from the quilt to "twelve o'clock," creating a 45° fold at the corner (diagram 27).

diagram 27

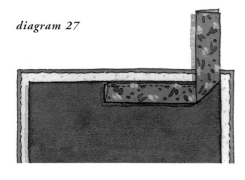

4 Fold the binding back down to "six o'clock," aligning the raw edge of the binding to the raw edge of the quilt. The fold created on the binding at the top should be the same distance away from the seam as the width of the finished binding. i.e. ½ in/1.25 cm from seam line to fold (diagram 28).

diagram 28

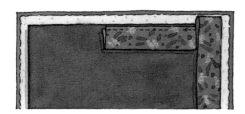

5 Start stitching the binding to the quilt at the same point the previous stitching stopped, ¼ in/0.75 cm from the edge of the quilt top. Secure with backstitching, then continue to the next corner. Repeat the process at each corner.

6 Stop about 2 in/5 cm from where you started. Open out the fold on both ends of the binding, then seam the two ends together. Trim away the excess, refold, and finish applying the binding to the quilt.

7 Trim the excess wadding and backing fabric so that the distance from the stitching line equals, or is slightly wider than, that of the finished binding. Fold the binding over to the back, and hand stitch the folded edge of the binding to the quilt along the row of machine stitching just created. A miter will appear at the corners on the front and on the back of the binding. Slipstitch these in place (diagram 29).

diagram 29

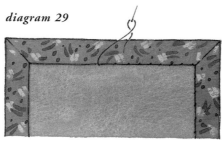

HANGING SLEEVE

If your quilt is a wallhanging or is to be exhibited it will need a hanging sleeve. A sleeve can be added after the quilt is completely finished, but a more secure and permanent sleeve can be added along with the binding. Stitch the binding to the front of the quilt and, before folding it over onto the back, add the sleeve.

1 Cut a piece of fabric, preferably matching the backing, to measure 10 in/25 cm by the width of the quilt. Make a 1 in/2.5 cm hem on both the short ends.

2 Fold the fabric in half along the length with wrong sides together. Center this on the back of the quilt, aligning the raw edges of the sleeve with the raw edges of the quilt. Secure with pins (diagram 30).

diagram 30

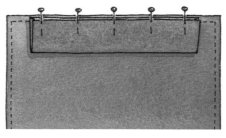

3 Turn the quilt over so the front is uppermost. Taking care to remove the pins as you approach them, stitch the sleeve to the quilt by stitching along the row of stitching made when applying the binding.

4 Finish hand stitching on the binding.

5 Lay the quilt on a flat surface with the back uppermost. Gently roll the top layer of the tube up to the top edge of the binding so it forms a fold along this edge. Secure with pins. Now smooth out the rest of the sleeve tube until it rests evenly on the back of the quilt (diagram 31).

diagram 31

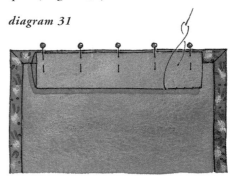

6 Stitch the sleeve to the back of the quilt along the fold at the bottom of the sleeve and at each end, so that when a rod is inserted it will not actually touch the back of the quilt, only the sleeve fabric. Take care that your stitches only go into the back and wadding of the quilt and are not visible on the front. Remove the pins. The sleeve is now stitched to the quilt and has a slight bulge in it. This bulge will allow room for a rod to go through the sleeve without distorting the quilt when it is hung.

LABELING

Your quilt should be signed, dated, and placed. This information provides a record for your own information, as well as for those in the future. A quilt that has this information on it is given more respect than one that does not.

The details can be incorporated on the quilt front or on a label on the back. A label can be simply handwritten with a permanent pen or made very elaborate with pieced, embroidered, or fabric painting. Another way of making an individual label is with the help of today's modern technology, the computer and printer.

Shadow Work

Designed by Dorothy Wood

Shadow work is a technique normally stitched on a small scale for cushions or wallhangings, but it works equally well on a quilt. The quilt top fabric is decorated with bright, colored squares of fabric, fixed in place with fusible webbing. A layer of fine muslin is laid on top, and the quilt sandwich is quilted by hand to keep the wonderful soft feel of the muslin. This single bed quilt is made entirely by hand, but because the stitches can be fairly large and there is no piecing, it only takes a few days to make.

NOTE

Choose deep colored fabrics for this quilt, as they will pale significantly with the layer of fine muslin on top, and make sure they are colorfast.

Finished size: 57½ x 89¼ in/146 x 226 cm

MATERIALS

All white fabrics used in this quilt are 59 in/150 cm wide. Colored fabrics are 45 in/115 cm wide

Colored squares: lime, deep pink, coral, turquoise, purple and fuchsia cotton fabric, 10 in/25 cm of each
Fusible webbing: 18 x 59 in /45.5 cm x 1.5 m
Baking parchment

Fine white muslin: 2¾ yds/2.40 m
White cotton: 2¾ yds/2.40 m
Backing: white, 2¾ yds/2.40 m
Wadding: 2 oz polyester, 60 x 96 in/152 x 243 cm
Quilting frame: 14 in/36 cm
White sewing thread
Tapestry needle
Stranded embroidery cotton: lime, deep pink, coral, turquoise, purple and fuchsia to match colored squares

ALTERNATIVE COLOR SCHEMES

1 This bold tie dye print produces a wonderful broken pattern on the quilt. Choose a fabric with plenty of white so that the splashed paint pattern is distinct. 2 Using a white fabric with large, brightly colored spots creates an unusual effect as the spots seem to float in the quilt. 3 Checks work well so long as the design is simple and the background color light enough so that the squares show quite clearly through the muslin. 4 The plain black fabric with deep grey stitching gives a simple Japanese look to the quilt and would be ideal in a boy's bedroom.

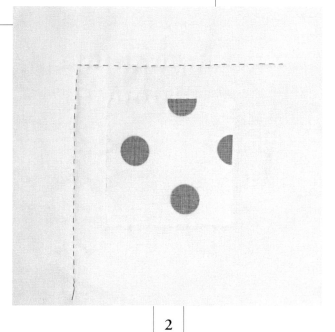

1

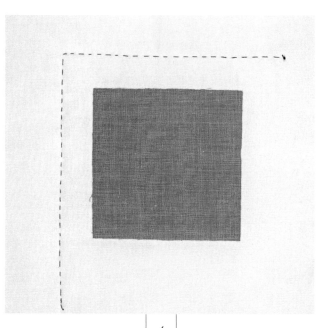

2

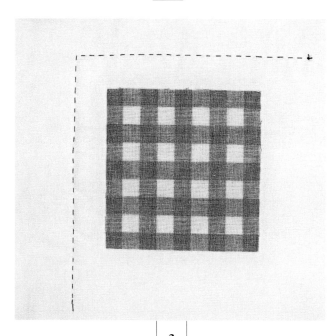

3

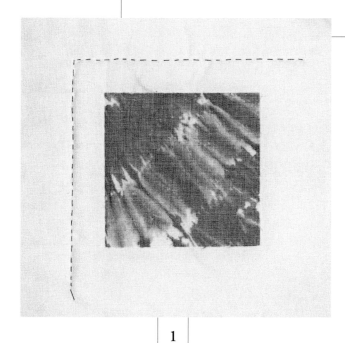

4

CUTTING

1 From each of the colored fabrics cut ten
4¾ in/12 cm squares. Place the squares side by side on
the fusible webbing. Cover with baking parchment
and iron with a medium hot iron. Peel off the backing
paper and separate the squares using a rotary cutter.

ASSEMBLING

1 Fold the white cotton fabric in half lengthwise and
crosswise and crease along the folds. Lay out flat.
Place four different fabric squares, fusible webbing
side down, in the center, leaving a ¾ in/2 cm gap
between each (diagram 1). Check that they are
absolutely straight, cover with baking parchment and
press with a medium iron to secure.

diagram 1

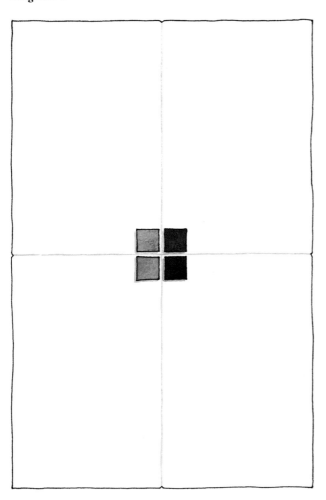

2 Measure out 6 in/15 cm to one side of the top
right square and position the first (top left) square of
the second block of four. Using a different combination of colors, position the next three squares with
the same gaps between. Check that they are straight
and press to secure.

3 Continue spacing the blocks of four squares
6 in/15cm apart until there are three blocks across
the width and five lengthwise, as shown in the quilt
assembly plan on page 18. Press the backing fabric
and lay flat. Place the wadding on top, then cover
with the quilt top. Finally place the fine muslin on
top. Pin through the layers, inserting two pins in each
colored square.

STITCHING

1 Lay the quilt flat. Fit a quilting frame around the
first block of squares and quilt around the edge of
each square using white sewing thread. The stitches
do not have to be tiny; 4 to 5 to the inch/2.5 cm is
ideal. Move the frame from block to block and quilt
around every square with white thread.

2 Using the tapestry needle and a quilter's rule as a
guide, score a line around one of the blocks
1 in/2.5 cm away from the colored squares. Choose a
color of stranded embroidery cotton to match one of
the squares. Quilt along the scored line using a single
strand of cotton (diagram 2). Repeat the process on
each block, changing the color each time.

diagram 2

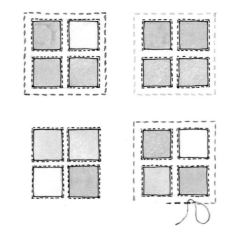

3 Lay the quilt flat. Score a line 6 in/15 cm away
from the colored blocks all the way around the edge.
Quilt with stranded cotton, changing the color each
time you start a new thread.

FINISHING

1 Fold back the muslin along the outside quilted line down one side. Fold the backing fabric underneath along the same line. Score a line on the white quilt top fabric, 1 in/2.5 cm out from the stitching. Trim this fabric and the wadding along this line (diagram 3). Repeat on all four sides.

2 Flatten out the muslin and backing fabric, then trim both ¾ in/2 cm from the edge of the wadding. Fold the backing fabric over the wadding along one side and turn the muslin under the quilt top fabric. Pin the edges together. Repeat on all four sides.

3 Slipstitch the edges together, taking care to stitch the corners securely (diagram 4).

diagram 3

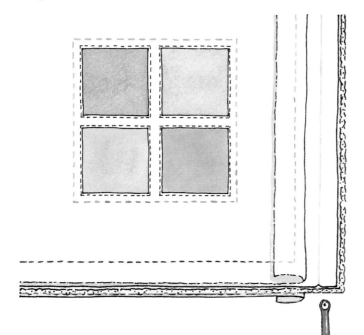

diagram 4

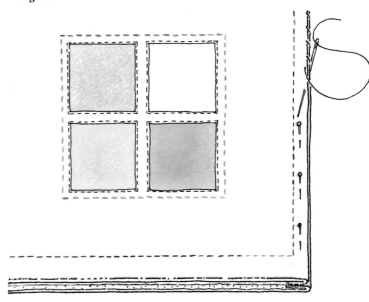

Round Peg, Square Hole

Designed by Rose Verney

This is an extremely simple design which works well on a small or large scale. I have used thirty-six squares in twelve colors to make this throw. You could change the size either by changing the dimensions of the squares and circles or by altering the number that are cut. The quilt does not have to be made square; it would work equally well as a bed quilt.

Finished size: 48 x 48 in/118 x 118 cm

MATERIALS
Plain fabric: fat quarters of each of 12 colors: I have used two greens, three blues, two yellows, three pinks, orange and apricot
Pair of compasses or 8 in/20 cm diameter plate
Backing: blue cotton, 52 x 52 in/128 x 128 cm

Wadding: 2 oz, 52 x 52 in/128 x 128 cm
Small buttons: 25
Fabric marking pencil
Crochet cotton: white
Fabric marking pencil
Binding: one fat quarter of a thirteenth color: I have used lilac

ALTERNATIVE COLOR SCHEMES

1 The palest of pastels makes a fresh and summery quilt made even prettier with white or pale pink stitching. 2 I adore stripes; lots of these are shirtings, easy to find at yard sales. Arrange the directions of the stripes differently. 3 A collection of predominantly black prints from my scrap bag makes a bold, dramatic color scheme. 4 Dark rich colors which are subtle variations on rust, chestnut and olive look great with black stitching.

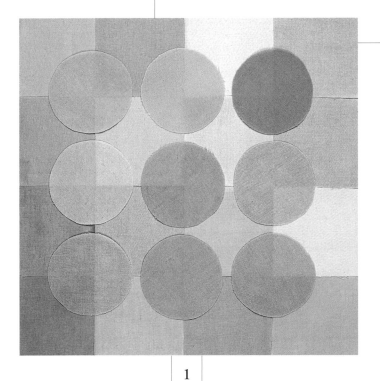

1

2

3

4

CUTTING

1 Cut three 8 in/20 cm squares from each of the 12 plain colored cottons.

2 Cut nine 8 in/20 cm circles (make a paper circle template with a compass, or use a plate and draw around it) from nine of the 12 plain colors.

3 For the border, using the leftovers of all the colors, cut pieces measuring 2¾ in/7 cm deep and anything from 1 to 6 in/2 to15 cm wide (diagram 1).

diagram 1

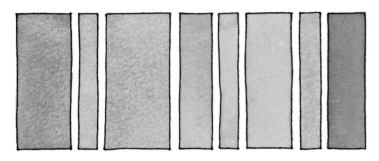

NOTE You can cut lots of these in advance, but I find it easiest to cut and join at the same time – start joining the pieces, then keep cutting and adding more until you have four strips of joined pieces measuring 2¾ x 47¾ in/7 x 118 cm – join them in any order: enjoy trying out different colors next to each other!

STITCHING

1 Pick out six squares each in a different color and stitch them together in a strip, taking a ¼ in/0.75 cm seam allowance. Press the seams open.

2 Stitch together the remaining six colors in the same way.

3 Do this twice more, using the colors in the same order as steps 1 and 2. (This way you will avoid finding any squares of the same color falling next to each other.) Press the seams open. Join the six strips as shown in diagram 2. As you will see, the two center strips are upside down. Press open all the seams.

diagram 2

4 Place the nine circles over the joins following the quilt assembly plan on page 24. Be sure to place the circles in such a way that each of the nine colors falls on four different colors, i.e. not on a square of the same color – this is quite easy! Pin and baste, keeping the basting stitches at least ½ in/1.5 cm from the raw edges.

5 Turn in ⅛ in/3 mm on each circle and hem, turning in as you go and using the needle to help you achieve a smooth curve. Press again, making sure all the seams on the back are flat.

FINISHING

1 If you haven't already done so, join the pieces for the striped border. When you have four border strips each 47¾ in/118 cm long, press all the seams open and stitch to the pieced top in a log cabin arrangement as shown in the quilt assembly diagram on page 24.

2 Spread the backing right side down on a flat surface, then smooth the wadding and the patchwork top, right side up, on top. Fasten together with safety pins or baste in a grid.

3 Using the white crochet cotton, quilt around the circles, and diagonally over the squares using big stitches. Use a fabric pencil to draw guidelines. Quilt an extra circle inside each big circle, in the center. (Use a glass or cup to guide you.)

4 Sew on 25 buttons, one at each junction and one in each circle, leaving a tuft of thread to tie into a knot. Trim the ends.

5 Cut the fabric for the binding, 2½ in/6.5 cm wide. Join the binding strips with diagonal seams to make a continuous length to fit all round the quilt. Use to bind the edges with a double-fold binding, mitered at the corners.

Apricot Wave

Designed by Rose Verney

The inspiration for this design came from a 1950s print dress my mother wore when I was a child, with a design of squiggles, polka dots and doodly lines. I have used a lovely, subtly textured white/yellow shot cotton as the base and have added two panels of pieced stripes at the sides, using all the colors of the central section, plus another pink for good measure.

Finished size: 45½ x 47¼ in/115 x 120 cm

MATERIALS
All fabrics used in the quilt top are 45 in/115 cm wide, 100% cotton

Central panel: pale yellow shot cotton, 1⅓ yds/1.20 m

Appliqué patches and striped panels: palest pink: ½ yd/50 cm; dark apricot: ½ yd/50 cm; light pink, mid pink, bright yellow, pinkish tan, apricot: fat quarters of each of these
Crochet cotton: white
Backing: mid pink, 1⅓ yds/1.20 m
Wadding: lightweight, 49 x 51 in/124 x 129 cm
Binding: dark apricot (included in allowance above)

ALTERNATIVE COLOR SCHEMES

1 A selection of my favorite greens set against a rich buttercup yellow makes a really sunny color scheme. 2 A cozy and colorful combination of warm pinks using wonderful shot cottons. 3 A sophisticated monochrome palette from charcoal grey through to a bleached-out green/grey, again in shot cottons. 4 Based on natural calico, these colors have a fresh, seaside feel.

1

2

3

4

CUTTING

1 Cut the central panel from the yellow fabric, 47¼ x 24¼ in/120 x 62 cm.

2 Make templates using the diagrams on pages 34 and 35 enlarged to full size. Cut the appliqué shapes from the templates, following the arrows for the direction of the grain of the fabric. There are eleven lines of appliqué and I have used five different fabrics twice, and the dark apricot for the center line of "U" shapes.

3 Cut thick and thin strips randomly from all colors for the two side panels, except the dark apricot, each 11 in/28 cm long. The thin stripes vary between 1 and 1¾ in/2.5 and 4.5 cm and the thick stripes from 2 to 3½ in/5 to 8.5 cm, including seam allowance. You will need approximately 17 wide strips and about the same number of narrow strips for each panel, depending on the widths. Vary the widths slightly and mix the colors as you like.

STITCHING

1 Pin the appliqué shapes to the central panel, centering them between the two sides of the panel and spacing the rows evenly, following the quilt assembly plan on page 30. Baste all the shapes on, keeping your stitches at least ⅜ in/1 cm from the raw edge.

NOTE The "S" shapes need to be positioned so that they overlap slightly; then when they have been hemmed they will be the right space apart. The spaces between the shapes should be similar but don't have to be exact.

2 Turn under about ⅛ in/2 to 3 mm and hem around the edges. Turn the edge in as you stitch, using your needle to help make smooth curves (diagram 1). Press, leaving the basting thread in place.

diagram 1

3 Using the white crochet cotton, work running stitches around the edge of each shape, about ⅛ in/ 3 mm from the hemmed edge. Press again and remove basting stitches.

4 Stitch the thick and thin stripes together for the two side panels, using a ¼ in/0.75 cm seam. They should each measure 47¼ in/120 cm long. Press all the seams open, trimming them if necessary to make the work lie flat. Stitch the two side panels to the center panel, using a ¼ in/0.75 cm seam. Press the seams towards the center.

FINISHING

1 Spread the backing right side down on a flat surface; then smooth the wadding and the patchwork top, right side up, on top. Fasten together with safety pins or baste in a grid.

2 Quilt through all layers, using the same thread as for the decorative stitching on the appliqué. Stitch a vertical line down each side of the central panel and ad lib horizontally (diagram 2).

diagram 2

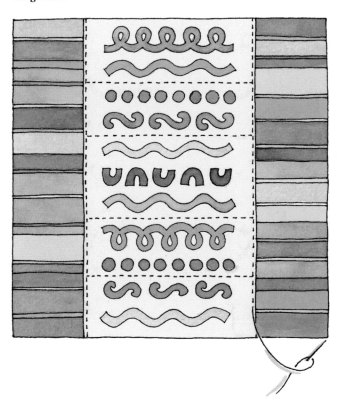

3 For the binding, cut strips of dark apricot fabric 1½ in/4 cm wide, either straight or bias cut, and join to make a continuous length to fit all round the quilt; then use to bind the edges with a single-fold binding, mitered at the corners.

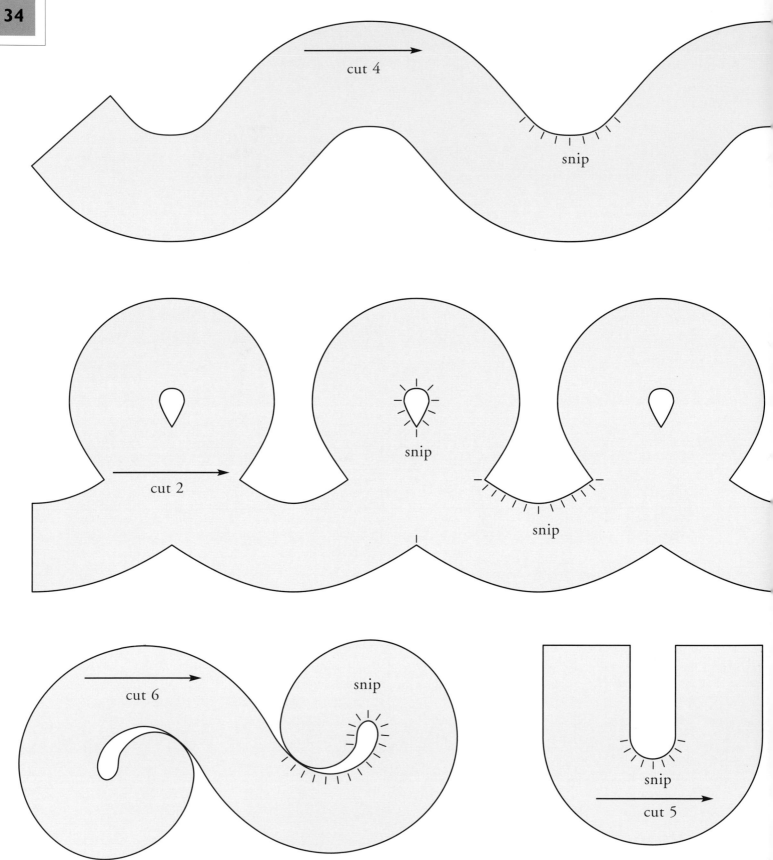

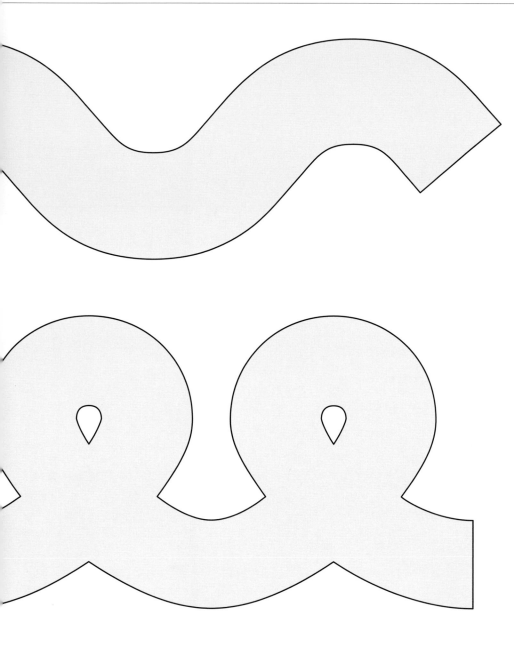

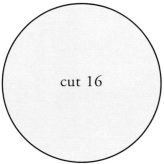

cut 16

All templates are 70% of full size. Enlarge on a photocopier.

Arrows show straight grain of fabric. Snip all inner curves and corners as indicated. Approximately ⅛ in/3 mm has been allowed for hems.

Jouy Medallion Wallhanging

Designed by Rosemary Wilkinson

Toile de Jouy fabric with its different cameos of idyllic country life is chosen as the centerpiece of this medallion quilt. The measurements given are based on the diamond cut from the largest of these cameos – other fabrics may need different measurements, so the quilt is designed with adaptable sizes and piecing patterns.

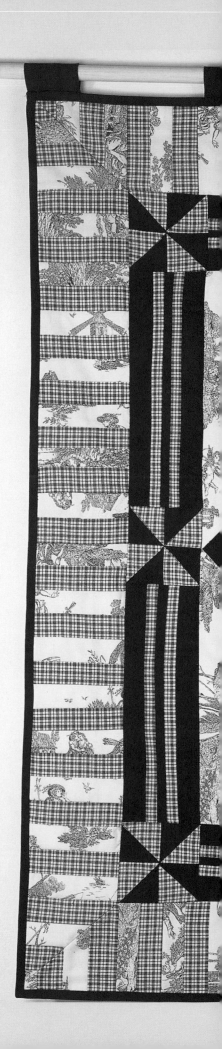

Finished size: 37 x 37 in/93 x 93 cm

MATERIALS
Feature fabric and backing: 2½ yds/2.20 m pink and white toile de Jouy, 56 in/144 cm wide. The amount is generous to allow for the cutting of the central square.
Checked fabric: red and white, 1 yd/1 m, 56 in/144 cm wide

Red fabric: 32 in/80 cm, 41 in/104 cm wide
Dressmaker's pattern paper: 1 sheet
Middle fabric: 1¼ yds/1 m white lawn, 41 in/104 cm wide
Bamboo pole or wooden dowel rod: 41 in/104 cm long
Two cup hooks

ALTERNATIVE COLOR SCHEMES

Choose the feature fabric first, then pick out two complementary fabrics. 1 This cat and mouse novelty print makes a fun design for a child's bedroom. 2 Choose the brightest colors from the botanical motifs to keep this design lively. 3 Mix and match muted florals to make a calm design perfect for a bedroom. 4 Plates taken from a novelty print matched with a lively check produce a crisp design.

CUTTING

1 Find the best motif on the toile de Jouy. Find the vertical center, fold and lightly press. Find the horizontal center, fold and lightly press. Open out, then measure an equal distance from the center in each direction, so that you are showing all of the motif, and mark. For the piece shown, I measured 8 in/22 cm. Using a ruler, align the marks and cut out the diamond shape. The sides of the square measure 12½ in/31 cm.
Reserve the remainder for the triangles and the backing.

2 From the checked fabric, cut a strip across the width, 3 in/7.5 cm deep; then cross-cut into four rectangles, 12½ x 3 in/31 x 7.5 cm;
cut 6 strips across the width, 1 in/2.5 cm deep;
cut 16 squares, 3 in/7.5 cm, for the pinwheels.

3 From the red fabric, cut a rectangle, 12 x 3 in/ 30 x 7.5 cm; then cross-cut into four squares;
cut 6 strips across the width, 1½ in/4 cm deep;
cut 3 strips across the width, 1 in/2.5 cm deep;
cut 16 squares, 3 in/7.5 cm, for the pinwheels;
cut 4 strips across the width, 1½ in/4 cm deep for the binding;
cut 1 strip across the width, 5 in/12.5 cm deep for the tabs.

STITCHING

1 Stitch one red 3 in/7.5 cm square to each end of one of the checked 12½ in/31 cm rectangles. Repeat. Press the seams towards the corner squares.

2 Stitch one of the checked 12½ in/31 cm rectangles to one side of the center toile de Jouy square. Stitch another to the opposite side of the square.

3 Stitch one of the strips made in Step One to the third side of the square and repeat with the remaining strip. Press the seams away from the center square.

4 Place the pattern paper underneath the square, so that one side rests along a diagonal. Work out where the apex of a right-angled trangle will be and mark (diagram 1). Measure one side and add 1¼ in/3.5 cm. Cut two squares from toile de Jouy to this measurement, then sub-cut both on the diagonal.

diagram 1

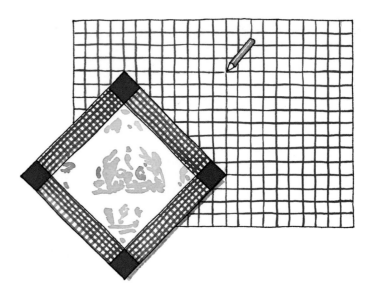

5 Stitch one triangle to one side of the central square and a second to the opposite side. Press the seams towards the striped fabric.

6 Stitch the remaining two triangles to the opposite sides and press as before.

7 Take the 6 red strips, 1½ in/4 cm deep, the 6 checked strips, 1 in/2.5 cm deep and the 3 narrower red strips, 1 in/2.5 cm deep. Stitch together along the long sides in the sequence shown in diagram 2. You will have three five-bar strips.

diagram 2

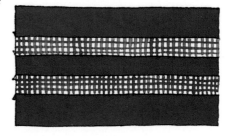

8 Stitch eight pinwheels using the 3 in/7.5 cm squares of red and checked fabric and following the method in Step 2 of adding the borders to the Sawtooth Stars quilt on page 59. Trim the pinwheel sides to fit the depth of the five-bar strips.

9 Stitch one pinwheel to one end of one of the five-bar strips. Press the seam away from the pinwheel. Match the center of the pinwheel to the center of one edge of the central square, mark the edge of the square on the five-bar strip, add a ¼ in/0.75 cm allowance and cut the strip (diagram 3).

diagram 3

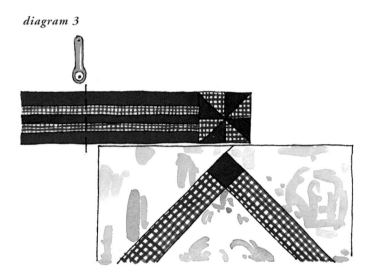

10 Stitch the five-bar strip to the other side of the pinwheel, press, match to the central square, add the seam allowance and cut as before.

11 Stitch a pinwheel to either end of these two strips. Press the seams away from the pinwheels. Repeat to form another strip of three pinwheels.

12 Repeat steps 9 and 10 but don't add the seam allowance. Stitch these strips to the top and bottom of the central square. Stitch the remaining two strips to the sides of the central square.

ADDING THE BORDERS

1 Cut 6 strips, 1½ in/4 cm deep, across the width of the checked fabric. Repeat on the toile de Jouy. You may not get full strips from the toile de Jouy, depending on how it was cut for the central medallion.

2 Place one strip of checked fabric with one of toile de Jouy, right sides together, and stitch down one long edge, taking the usual seam allowance. Repeat with the remaining strips; then cross-cut these strips into 4¼ in/11 cm rectangles.

3 Measure the pieced top through the center from side to side, then add 8½ in/22 cm to this measurement. Stitch the rectangles together along the longer sides, alternating fabrics to make four strips to the measured length. Slightly adjust the seams between the strips if necessary to make the exact measured length.

4 Stitch the borders to the pieced top and miter the corners.

FINISHING

1 Cut a piece 1¼ yds/1 m square from the toile de Jouy for the backing and from the white lawn.

2 Spread the backing right side down on a flat surface. Smooth the white fabric and the pieced top, right side up, on top. Fasten together with safety pins or baste in a grid.

3 Machine quilt "in-the-ditch" around the central medallion, on either side of the five-bar strips and diagonally across the pinwheels.

4 Join the binding strips into one length long enough to go all around the quilt and use to bind the quilt with a double-fold binding, mitered at the corners.

5 Fold the 5 in/12.5 cm strip for the tabs in half along the length, right sides together. Stitch down the long side taking the usual seam allowance; then turn right side out and press with the seam in the middle.

6 Cross-cut into five 4½ in/11.5 cm pieces. Fold in half with the seam on the outside. Stitch across the short end. Turn inside out and press. Lay evenly across the top of the wallhanging and stitch in place.

7 Thread onto the bamboo pole and hang from cup hooks.

Flower Strippy

Designed by Frances de Rees

Placing striped patterns next to traditional florals emphasizes the strip design of this easily pieced quilt. Ten different prints are used here, so this quilt could be a good excuse to finally use up some of those scrap fabrics, although you do need a full width of each. The strips are cut with a rotary cutter, quickly machine-pieced and simply hand-quilted using the strips as a guide.

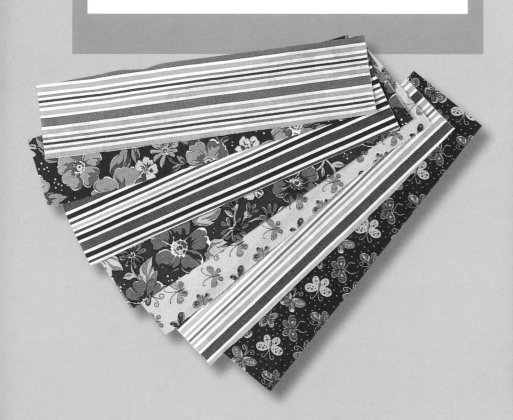

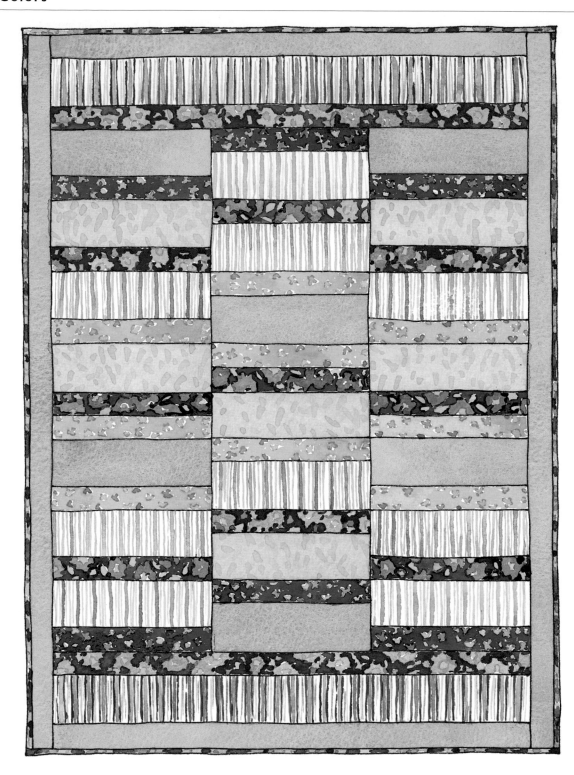

Finished size: 61½ x 45½ in/156 x 116 cm

MATERIALS
All fabrics in the quilt top are 45 in/ 115 cm wide
100% cotton

Large strips: prints **a**, **c** and **e**, 9 in/23 cm of each;
prints **f**, **i** and **j**, 4½ in/11.50 cm of each

Small strips: prints **b** and **g**, 7½ in/19.50 cm of each;
prints **d** and **h**, 5 in/13 cm of each
Binding: an extra 8 in/20 cm of one of the strip
fabrics: I used print **h**
Border: an extra 15 in/40 cm of one of the strip
fabrics: I used print **c**
Backing: 3½ yds/3.25 m
Wadding: 64½ x 49½ in/166 x 126 cm
Quilting thread: ivory

ALTERNATIVE COLOR SCHEMES

1 Using darker hues of the same color frames the lighter shades and shows them to their best advantage. 2 The subtle effect of using similar red tones gives this a warm abstract feel. 3 The vertical stripes included here draw the eye to the picture panels. 4 The clash of patterns is effective because of the similarity of tone and color shades.

1

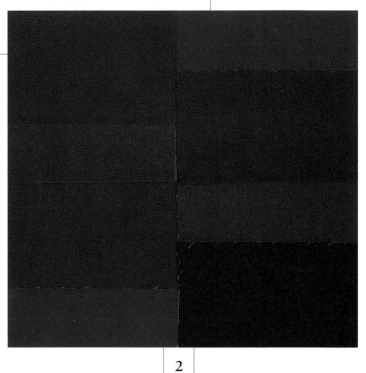

2

3

4

CUTTING

1 From prints **a**, **c** and **e**, cut 2 strips across the width of the fabric, 4½ in/11.5 cm deep.

2 From prints **f**, **i** and **j**, cut 1 strip across the width of the fabric, 4½ in/11.5 cm deep.

3 From prints **b** and **g**, cut 3 strips across the width of the fabric, 2½ in/6.5 cm deep.

4 From prints **d** and **h**, cut 2 strips across the width of the fabric, 2½ in/6.5 cm deep.

5 From the border fabric, cut 5 strips across the width, 2¾ in/7 cm deep.

6 From the binding fabric, cut 5 strips across the width, 3½ in/9 cm deep.

> NOTE   It may help to pin scraps of the off-cuts in the correct sequence as shown in diagram 1 on a piece of paper. This is useful reference to avoid adding a strip in the wrong order.

STITCHING

1 Put to one side two **a** strips and two **b** strips. Arrange the remaining strips in order of assembly as shown in diagram 1. Stitch the strips together along the width of the fabric, taking a ¼ in/0.75 cm seam allowance. Press all the seams in the same direction.

diagram 1

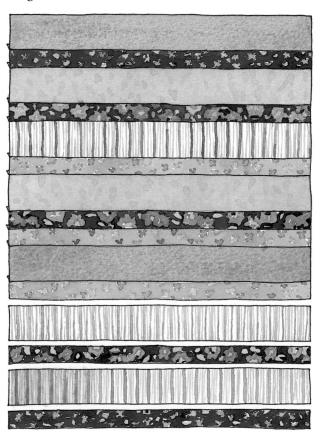

c
d
e
b
f
g
e
h
g
c
g
i
h
j
d

2 Using a rotary cutter and ruler, trim the edges of the panel to even them. Fold the stitched panel in half widthwise and measure across the width at the top. Divide this measurement into three; then cut the panel lengthwise into three equal panels (diagram 2).

diagram 2

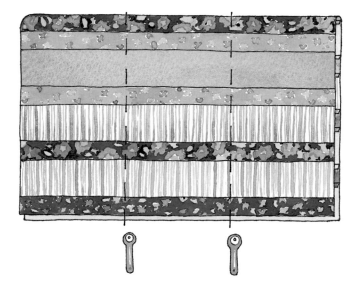

3 Turn the central panel upside down; then replace between the two side panels. Stitch the three panels together, taking the usual seam allowance and aligning all horizontal seams where appropriate (diagram 3). The horizontal seams are now lying in opposite directions and this helps the seams lie flatter. Do not

diagram 3

press the seams open as this would weaken the seams, and also seams pressed to one side make it easier to quilt "in-the-ditch" at a later stage.

4 Add one strip **b** to the top and one strip **b** to the bottom of this pieced panel. Repeat with the two **a** strips. Trim the edges even with the rest of the panel.

ADDING THE BORDERS

1 Measure the pieced panel through the center from side to side; then trim the two shorter border strips to this measurement. Stitch to the top and bottom of the panel.

2 Join the remaining three border strips into one length. Measure the pieced top through the center from top to bottom; then cut two strips to this measurement from the joined piece. Stitch to the sides of the panel (diagram 4).

diagram 4

FINISHING

1 Cut the wadding and backing fabric 3 in/7.5 cm larger than the quilt top on all sides. Spread the backing right side down on a flat surface; then smooth the wadding and the pieced top, right side up, on top. Fasten together with safety pins or baste in a grid.

2 Quilt "in-the-ditch" along all seams either by hand or machine.

3 Join the binding strips to fit the long sides of the quilt. Fold in half and press. Pin one strip to the side of the quilt, aligning raw edges. Stitch; then fold over to the back of the quilt and slip stitch in place. Repeat with the second side; then do the same for the top and bottom of the quilt.

Eight Pointed Stars

Designed by Katharine Guerrier

Eight pointed star blocks are made in a range of patterned pastels set into crisp white sashing strips with corner posts. Some of the star blocks are made with extra detail in the centers, providing interest and variety and linking the fabrics used in the stars. A vibrant pink is used for the binding. The quilting is done on a "Gammil" long arm machine by Beryl Cadman of "Custom Quilting Limited."

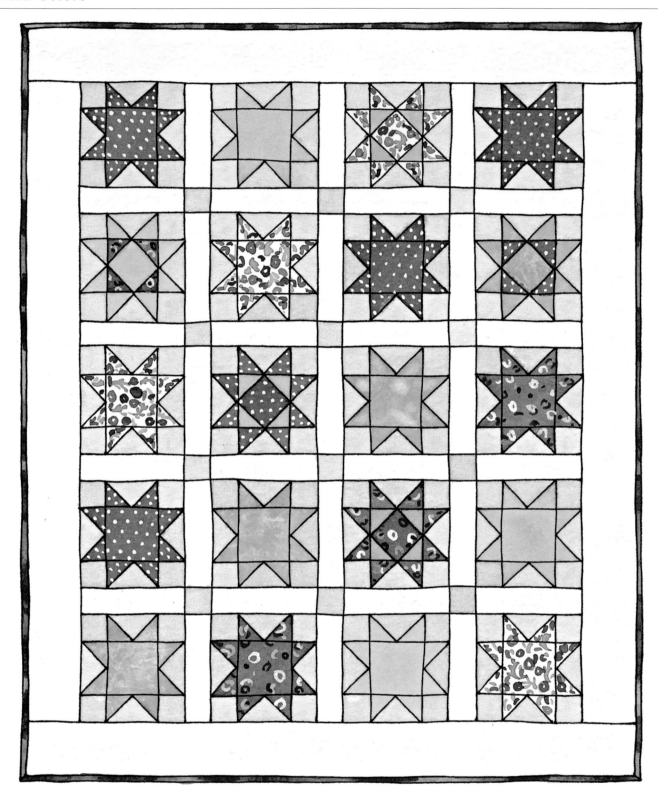

Finished size: 48 x 58 in/122 x 147 cm

MATERIALS
All fabrics in the quilt top are 45 in/115 cm wide
100% cotton
Star fabrics: three pink and two green fat quarters in
a range of patterns: spots, floral or marbled

Background to the stars and corner posts: yellow,
1¼ yds/1 m
Sashing, backing and borders: white, 3¾ yds/
3½ m
Binding: magenta pink, ½ yd/50 cm
Wadding: 54 x 64 in/137 x 163 cm
Quilting thread: pastel variegated thread

ALTERNATIVE COLOR SCHEMES

1 The contrast in this block between the star fabric and the background is created by the difference in scale of the prints. 2 For maximum visual impact, team black with a highly contrasting bright color. 3 Use solid colors to emphasize the geometric shapes in the block for a good graphic effect. 4 There is a wide range of batik fabrics in subtle colors available to quiltmakers which will give your blocks a contemporary appeal.

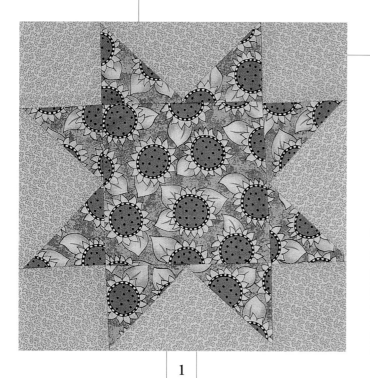

1

2

3

4

CUTTING

1 From the star fabrics, cut one 4½ in/11.5 cm square for the center; cut eight 2½ in/6 cm squares for the star points. This is enough for one block; you will need 20 sets total.

2 From the yellow background, cut four 2½ in/6 cm squares for the corners; cut four 4½ x 2½ in/11.5 x 6 cm rectangles for the star points. This is enough for one block; you will need 20 sets total.

3 For the "Diamond in a Square" detail on some block centers, in addition to the 4½ in/11.5 cm squares just cut, cut four 2½ in/6 cm squares in one of the other star fabrics. You will need 5 sets total.

4 Before cutting out the sashing strips from the white fabric, cut four strips for the borders, 5¼ in/ 13.5 cm wide and 49 in/124.5 cm long, and make up the backing piece 56 x 66 in/142 x 168 cm.

5 From the remaining white sashing fabric, cut 31 strips, 8½ x 2½ in/22 x 6 cm.

6 From the remaining yellow fabric, cut twelve 2½ in/6 cm squares for the corner posts.

7 From the magenta pink, cut strips of binding, 2½ in/6 cm deep to a total length of 215 in/547 cm.

STITCHING

To make one star block:

1 Place one of the 2½ in/6 cm squares of star fabric over a yellow 2½ x 4½ in/ 6 x 11.5 cm rectangle, aligning the lefthand side and with right sides together. Draw a diagonal line as shown in diagram 1 and stitch on this line. Cut the corners away ¼ in/0.75 cm from the stitching line.

diagram 1

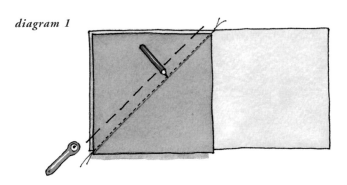

2 Open out and press the seam towards the triangle.

3 Place a second 2½ in/6 cm square of star fabric over the rectangle, aligning the righthand side, draw a diagonal line and stitch as before.

4 Trim and press as before. Repeat three more times to make four star point units altogether (diagram 2).

diagram 2

5 To make the center detail (on five blocks only), place two of the 2½ in/6 cm squares, which you have cut from one of the other star fabrics at opposite sides of the center square, right sides together and aligning corners, draw two diagonal lines as shown in diagram 3 and stitch along these lines. Cut away the corners ¼ in/ 0.75 cm from the stitching.

diagram 3

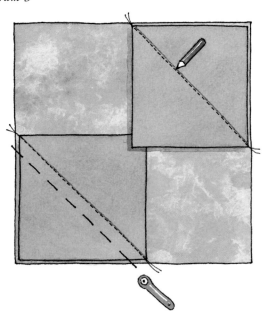

6 Open out and press the seams towards the triangles.

7 Repeat on the remaining opposite sides of the center square with the other two matching 2½ in/6 cm squares. Open out and press as before (diagram 4).

diagram 4

8 Stitch the blocks together as illustrated in diagrams 5a and 5b, matching points where necessary. Make four blocks in each of the five star fabrics, adding the center detail to one in each set (twenty blocks altogether; five with center detail).

diagram 5a

diagram 5b

9 Lay out the blocks on a flat surface, following the quilt assembly plan on page 50.

10 Stitch four columns of five blocks together with a white sashing strip between each block.

11 Stitch the short sides of five sashing strips with a yellow corner post between each. Repeat twice to make three sets of sashing strips and corner posts.

12 Stitch the four columns of blocks together with a set of sashing strips between each column.

13 Stitch border strips to the two longer sides of the quilt, press the seams; then stitch the remaining two border strips to the top and bottom of the quilt.

FINISHING

1 Spread the backing right side down on a flat surface; then smooth the wadding and the pieced top, right side up, on top. Fasten together with safety pins or baste in a grid.

2 Quilt by hand or machine in the desired quilting pattern. The quilt photographed was quilted on a long arm machine in an edge-to-edge "hearts and daisies" pattern using pastel variegated thread.

3 Join the binding strips and use to bind the quilt with a double-fold binding, mitered at the corners.

Sawtooth Stars

Designed by Maggie Wise

This vibrant little quilt is very easy and quick to make using a rotary cutter and quick piecing techniques. You could literally piece it in one weekend and quilt it in another.

Finished size: 72 x 72 in/183 x 183 cm

MATERIALS
All fabrics used in the quilt top are 45 in/115 cm wide, 100% cotton

Star backgrounds and pinwheel borders: white, 2 yds/1.70 m
Star points and pinwheel borders: multi-colored fabric, 1⅝ yds/1.40 m

Star centers: 8 bright prints, 6 in/15 cm of each color
Star setting triangles: 4 very pale prints, 24 in/60 cm of each
Inner border and binding: green spot fabric, 1¼ yds/1.10 m
Backing: very pale print, 75½ x 75½ in/192 x 192 cm
Wadding: 2 oz polyester, 75½ x 75½ in/192 x 192 cm

ALTERNATIVE COLOR SCHEMES

This quilt is made up of a number of fabrics in a general range of colors with the pinwheels and stars establishing the tone. The background color is also important for setting off these other fabrics. The alternative schemes below show how you can achieve different moods for the quilt. 1 Homespun: using muted checks and small florals. 2 Provençal: crisp flowery fabrics. 3: Sweet liberty: using soft cotton lawn fabrics. 4 Forest green: a strong collection of leaf designs and bold greens.

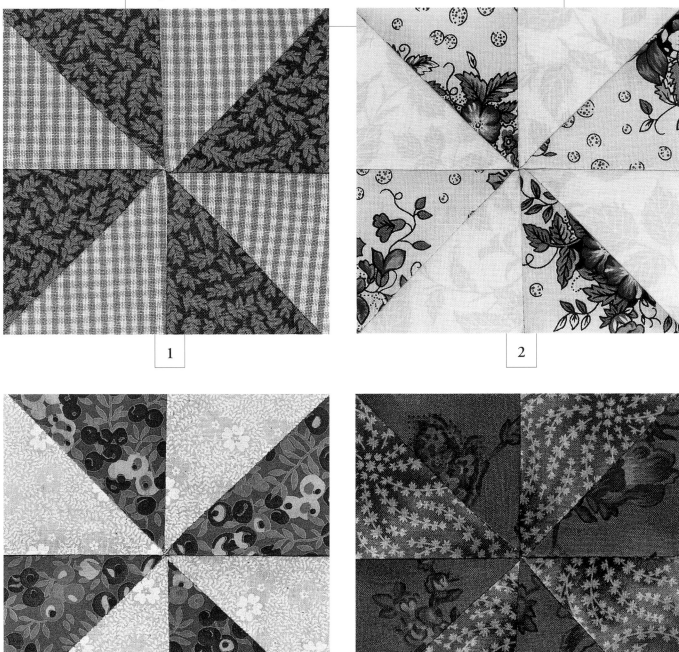

CUTTING

1 For the star blocks, cut:

36 x 6½ by 3½ in/16.5 x 9 cm rectangles from white for star points (**a**);

72 x 3½ in/9 cm squares from multi-colored fabric for star points (**b**);

36 x 3½ in/9 cm squares from eight bright prints for block centers, (**d**);

36 x 3½ in/9 cm squares from white for corners (**e**);

20 x 10 in/25.5 cm squares from four pale prints (cut 5 squares from each color); sub-cut each square once diagonally to make the setting triangles.

2 For the inner border, from green spot fabric cut 2 strips across the width and 2 in/5 cm deep. Piece together along the short edges; then cut:
2 strips, 51½ x 2 in/133 x 5 cm for the top and bottom;
2 strips, 54½ x 2 in/141 x 5 cm for the sides.

3 For the outer pinwheel borders, cut:
104 x 3⅛ in/8 cm squares from multi-colored fabric;
104 x 3⅛ in/8 cm squares from white.

NOTE

If you place the two fabrics right sides together and press before you cut the squares for the pinwheels, they will be ready for marking and stitching.

4 For the binding: cut 8 x 2 in/5 cm strips.

STITCHING

1 To make the four-patch centers, place two bright print squares (**d**), right sides together and stitch, taking a ¼ in/0.75 cm seam allowance. Press the seam towards the darker fabric. Repeat with two more squares.

2 Stitch the two-square units together matching the center seam carefully. (The way they are pressed will help them to nestle nicely.) This makes the center of the block (diagram 1). Repeat to make a total of nine.

diagram 1

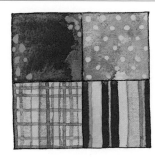

3 To make the star point units (**c**), take one white piece (**a**) and two multi-colored pieces (**b**). Mark each piece (**b**) with a diagonal line from corner to corner. Place one piece (**b**) on one piece (**a**), right sides together, aligned to one end (diagram 2).

diagram 2

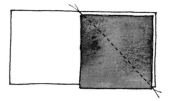

4 Stitch diagonally along the marked line; then trim back the corner to a ¼ in/0.75 cm seam. Open out and press the seam towards the darker fabric.

5 Repeat on the opposite end of (**a**) using the second piece (**b**). This makes unit **c**, and you will need to make four of these units for each star (36 in total).

6 To make the Sawtooth Star block, take four (**c**) units, one four-patch center and four (**e**) pieces. Assemble the star in strip units as shown in diagram 3. Repeat to make a total of nine.

diagram 3

7 Take two setting triangles in different colors. These are cut oversize; then trimmed to give perfect sized blocks. Stitch one to each side of the center block using a ¼ in/0.75 cm seam allowance. Press the seams away from the center.

8 Take two more setting triangles, again in different colors, and stitch one to each of the remaining sides of the star block. Press the seams away from the center.

9 The next stage is trimming. Line up the side of the center square with the 45 degree line on your ruler. Ensure a generous ¼ in/0.75 cm allowance projects beyond the star block and trim (diagram 4).

diagram 4

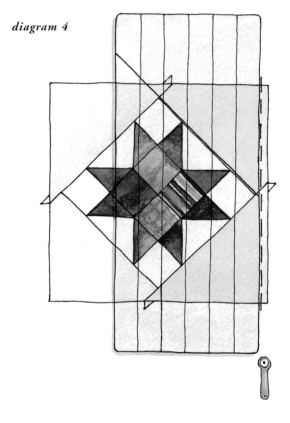

10 Join the blocks into three rows of three blocks as shown in the quilt assembly plan on page 56. Stitch the blocks into rows; then stitch the rows together. This makes the center section.

ADDING THE BORDERS

1 Stitch the top and bottom inner borders to the center section, followed by the side inner borders as shown in the assembly plan. Trim level if necessary.

2 To make the pinwheel borders, take the 104 pairs of 3⅛ in/8 cm squares. Mark each pair diagonally; then stitch ¼ in/0.75 cm each side of the line. Cut on the marked line to make two half-square triangles. Piece these together to make pinwheel blocks (diagram 5).

diagram 5

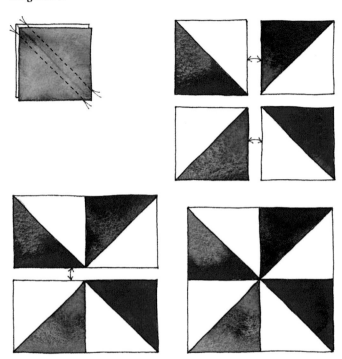

3 For the top and bottom borders stitch 12 pinwheel blocks together and join to the quilt. For the side borders use 14 blocks.

FINISHING

1 Give the backing and the pieced top a good press; then spread the backing right side down on a flat surface. Smooth the wadding and the pieced top, right side up, on top. Fasten together with safety pins or baste in a grid.

2 I did not need to mark the quilt. I quilted it free-hand by machine, in rows to form a water-like pattern. I wanted an all-over, but tranquil pattern that emphasized the watery colored fabrics I'd used to set the stars. I used a medium sized vermicelli pattern to emphasize the movement in the pinwheel border.

3 Join the binding strips into one length long enough to go all around the quilt and use to bind the quilt with a double-fold binding, mitered at the corners.

Glow Worms

Designed by Claire Higgott

The background for this quilt is quickly and easily made with free cut blocks, so there is very little measuring involved! The blocks have been arranged so that the colors shade from dark to light across the quilt, but they would also look good used randomly. The spirals (or glow worms!) bring the quilt to life and are bonded in place before stitching.

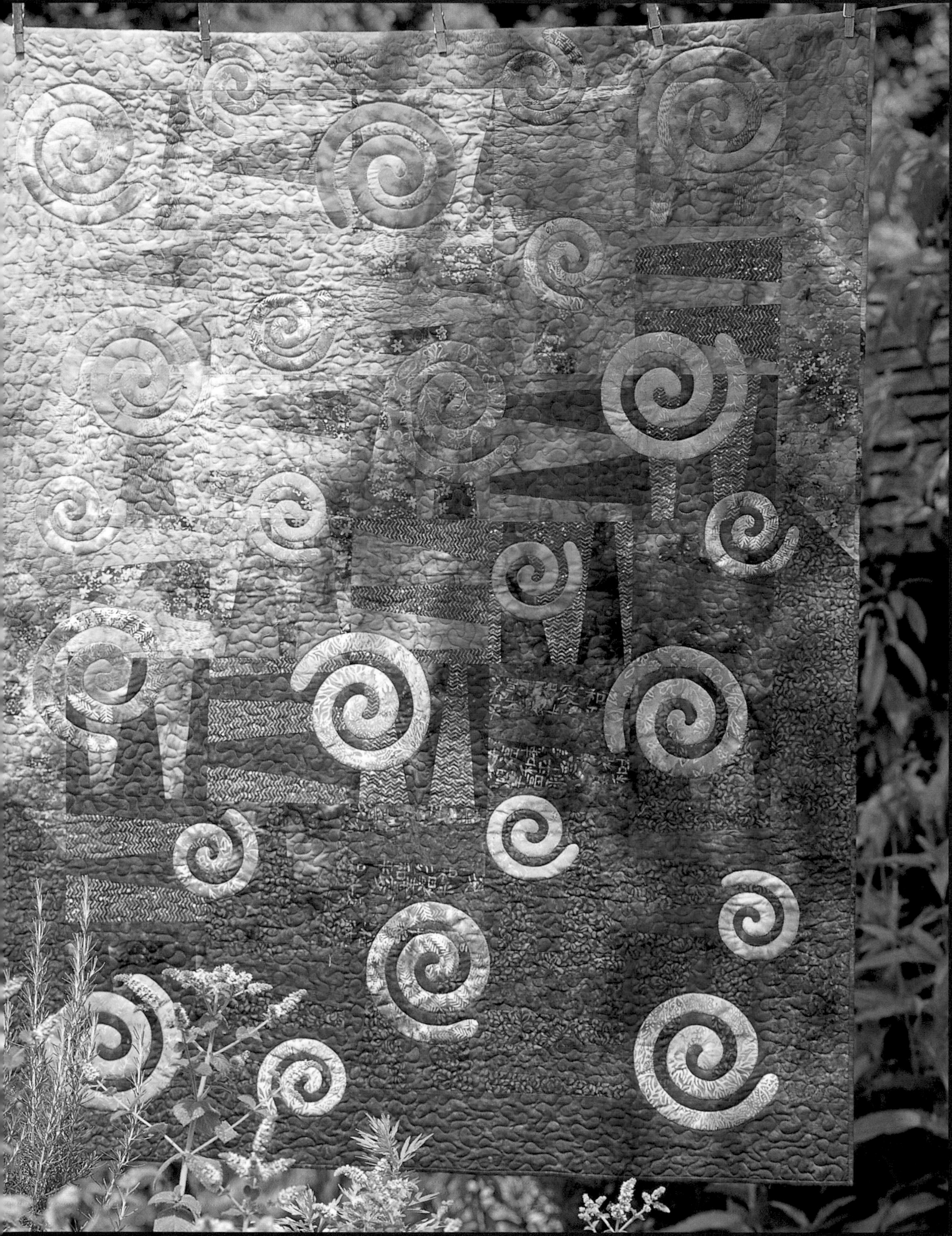

Quilt size: 50 x 66 in/122.5 x 161.5 cm

MATERIALS
All fabrics used in the quilt top are 45 in/115 cm
wide.

Batik fabrics for the blocks, borders and binding:
nine different blue shades, ½ yd/50 cm of each

Batik fabrics for the spirals: orange and green, 6 fat
quarters in total, or a variety of scraps (at least 9 in/
23 cm square for the large spirals and 6 in/15 in
square for the small spirals)
Fusible webbing: 1½ yds/1.50 m
"Stitch and Tear": 1 yd/1 m
Backing: navy blue print, 56 x 72 in/137.5 x 176.5 cm
Wadding: lightweight, 56 x 72 in/137.5 x 176.5 cm

ALTERNATIVE COLOR SCHEMES

1 Spots and stripes can swim before your eyes and cause all sorts of optical illusions, but here the neutral colors temper the effect and would suit a modern setting. 2 The blue floral fabrics, which are very similar in value, make a subtle background for the deep blue spirals. 3 The combination of black and white is always striking, and the scarlet spiral stands out graphically against the background. 4 Bright orange prints give this colorway a real zing.

1

2

3

4

CUTTING
(Cut strips selvage to selvage unless otherwise indicated.)

1 From each of the nine blue fabrics, cut a 5 in/ 12.5 cm strip for the borders and a 2 in/5 cm strip for the binding and set these aside.

2 Divide the rest of each of the blue fabrics into four equal pieces – they should measure 10 to 11 in/ 25.5 to 28 cm square – but this is not crucial! There should be thirty-six pieces total.

STITCHING
(Use a ¼ in/0.75 cm seam allowance throughout.)

1 Sort the thirty-six square-ish pieces into pairs. If you want to shade the background of the quilt, most of the pieces should be paired, so that the values are similar - light with light, medium with medium, dark with dark. However a few "crossover" pairs – light with medium and medium with dark – will help the shading process. Alternatively, you could pair the fabrics randomly.

2 Arrange each pair one on top of the other with right sides up and press together.

3 Take one of the pairs and place it on the cutting board. If they are fairly square it doesn't matter which way around they go. However, if one side is longer than the other make sure the longer side is closest to you. Using a rotary cutter and ruler – but without measuring – make four cuts through the two fabrics as shown by the dotted lines in diagram 1. The exact position and angle of the cuts will vary with each pair.

diagram 1

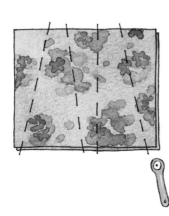

4 Carefully separate the top fabric pieces from the bottom fabric pieces, keeping them in the same order. Rearrange the strips so that pieces 1, 3 and 5 of the top fabric are teamed up with 2 and 4 of the bottom fabric, and 1,3 and 5 of the bottom fabric are teamed with 2 and 4 of the top fabric. These will be the first two blocks (diagram 2).

diagram 2

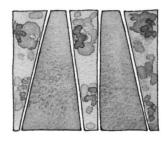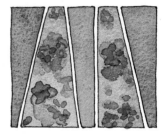

5 Stitch the four seams in each block and press the seams carefully to one side. Repeat with the remaining pairs to make a total of thirty-six blocks.

6 To complete the blocks, trim them all square. The precise size is not important, but they must all be the same! The blocks in my quilt were trimmed to 8½ in/21 cm square, but fabric widths do vary a little and you may find that yours are big enough to trim to 9 in/22 cm square.

7 Arrange thirty-five of the blocks in seven rows of five, following the quilt assembly plan on page 62 (save the last block to make a label for the back of the quilt). If you are shading the colors across the quilt, play with various layouts until you are happy with the arrangement.

8 Stitch the blocks in each row together, pressing the seams in opposite directions on alternate rows as you go; then stitch the rows together – the seams that were pressed in alternate directions should now butt together to ensure a good match. Press well.

ADDING THE BORDERS
If you have shaded your quilt top, follow steps 1 to 5; if you have randomly pieced the blocks, follow steps 6 to 9.

1 Pin the quilt top on a design board or lay it out flat. Using the 5 in/12.5 cm strips of fabric that you

set aside, arrange the various colors roughly around the edges – you may find it easier to cut the strips in half. Decide where to make the joins, so that the colors shade around the quilt in line, more or less, with the colors in the quilt top. This is not an exact science!

diagram 3

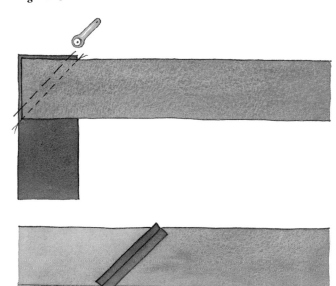

2 Measure the width of the quilt through the center and join enough pieces together to make the top and bottom border sections. The joins can be made at right angles in the usual way or at a 45 degree angle. The angles look good if they slant in the same direction as the shading. To make an angled join, position two strips at right angles to each other, with right sides together. Draw a line across the corner at 45 degrees and stitch on the line. Trim the excess fabric off the corner and press the seam open (diagram 3).

3 After joining the border sections, check the width and trim if necessary. Stitch the top and bottom border sections to the quilt top. Press the seams towards the borders.

4 Measure the length of the quilt including the borders and join enough 5 in/12.5 cm strips as before to make the side border sections.

5 After joining check the length and trim if necessary. Stitch the side border sections to the quilt. Press the seams towards the borders; then press the whole quilt top and proceed to applying the spirals.

6 Measure the width of the quilt through the center. Cut the 5 in/12.5 cm border strips to various lengths (anything between about 6 and 18 in/15 and 50 cm). Join enough pieces together (using the colors randomly) to make the top and bottom border sections. Press the seams open.

7 After joining, check the width and trim if necessary. Stitch the top and bottom border sections to the quilt top. Press the seams towards the borders.

8 Measure the length of the quilt including the borders and join enough pieces together as before to make the side border sections.

9 After joining check the length and trim if necessary. Stitch the side border sections to the quilt. Press the seams towards the borders; then press the whole quilt top.

APPLYING THE SPIRALS

1 Trace twelve large spirals and twelve small spirals from the templates on the opposite page onto the paper side of the fusible webbing.

2 Cut out around the outside of the spirals leaving a small margin around each one.

3 Iron the spirals onto the back of the green and orange fabrics: six large and six small in each color. Cut out along the lines.

4 Arrange the spirals on the quilt, and when you are happy with the layout, peel the paper backing off and iron them in place.

5 To avoid puckering, place a piece of "Stitch and Tear" behind each spiral; then stitch around the edges of the spirals to secure them. We used a zig-zag stitch and matching threads. Alternatively you could use a straight stitch, a satin stitch or a blanket stitch. You could also try decorative threads. Make an extra spiral and iron it onto some spare fabric so that you can experiment first.

6 After all the spirals have been stitched, remove the "Stitch and Tear" carefully from the back.

FINISHING

1 Spread the backing right side down on a flat surface, then smooth the wadding and the pieced top, right side up, on top. Fasten together with safety pins or baste in a grid.

2 Machine or hand quilt in the pattern of your choice.

NOTE "Glow Worms" has been machine quilted on "Bertha," the long arm quilting machine at "The Bramble Patch," with a large "vermicelli" pattern all over the background blocks. The spirals were simply outlined. Alternatively, you could quilt by hand or machine to emphasize the angled lines of the blocks.

3 Take the nine 2 in/5 cm strips of blue fabric and cut them into a variety of shorter lengths (anything from 6 to 18 in/15 to 50 cm long). Rejoin the sections of binding at 45 degrees as for the border strips. You can either shade the colors to flow around the quilt or join randomly (as with the border strips). Trim the excess fabric off the corners; then press the seams open.

4 Fold the binding in half along the length and use to bind the quilt with a double-fold binding mitered at the corners.

5 Don't forget to add a label to your quilt!

templates - full size

Aurora

Designed by Jean Hunt

The inspiration for this lap quilt came from wonderful fabric, which is produced in a spectrum of glowing colors. The block design developed from our attempts to use as many of the colors as possible in one quilt. After the quilting was completed, when we stood back and looked at it, we could see lots of little sailing boats on a higgledy-piggledy sea! This was an unexpected bonus; however this depends on what fabric you use. Because it is made up of blocks, the quilt could easily be made larger by adding more blocks – but you will obviously need to buy more fabric. We used a twin needle sewing machine for the quilting, but this is optional.

Finished size: 36 x 48 in/93 x 122 cm

MATERIALS
All fabrics used in the quilt top are 45 in/115 cm wide, 100% cotton

Fabrics: 6 x ½ yd/50 cm of toning or graded fabrics, or 1 yd/1 m of "feature" fabric and 4 x ½ yd/50 cm of complementary fabric

Binding: 6 in/15 cm of fabric cut across the bolt
Stiff cardboard
Tracing or freezer paper
Quilter's pencil
Wadding: 2 oz polyester, 40 x 52 in/103 x 132 cm
Backing: cotton fabric, 40 x 52 in/103 x 132 cm
Variegated machine quilting thread

ALTERNATIVE COLOR SCHEMES

The triangle at the center of the block provides a "window" into which you could put a feature fabric if desired, but take care when using directional fabrics as the blocks are twisted around in different directions before being stitched together. A random all-over print would be fine. You could use either a contrast or a blend as the examples here show.

1

2

3

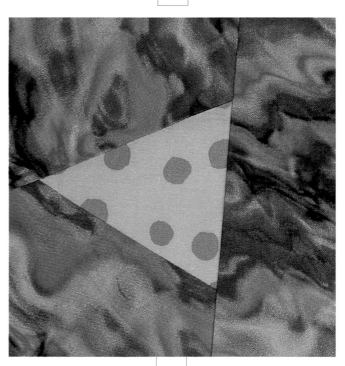

4

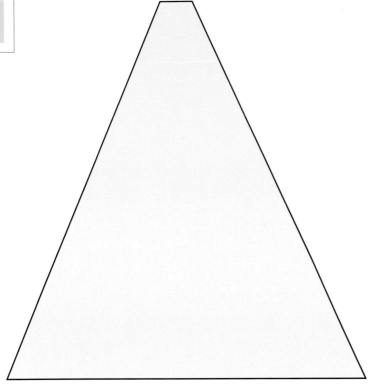

template

CUTTING

1 Trace off the triangle template above and stick to a piece of stiff card. Cut out from the card as accurately as possible. Note that the ¼ in/0.75 cm seam allowance is already included in the template.

2 Cut a 4 in/10 cm strip from your chosen central or feature fabric. Following the cutting plan (diagram 1), draw around the triangle template using a quilter's pencil. You will need 48 triangles altogether. Cut out the triangles.

diagram 1

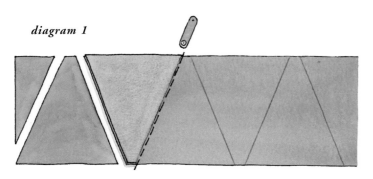

3 Cut the outer strips from the remaining fabrics using a rotary cutter. For each block you will need: two 3½ x 6 in/9 x 15 cm strips, one 3½"x 9 in/9 x 23 cm strip. Since there are 48 blocks, you will need to cut the above sets 48 times total. To save time, cut a long 3½ in/9 cm strip from your chosen fabric; then cut this to the desired length when required.

4 For the binding, cut the 6 in/15 cm strip into four 1½ in/3.75 cm strips.

STITCHING

1 Take one of the triangles and one 3½ x 6 in/9 x 15 cm strip. Place the strip right side up and lay the triangle on top, right side down, no more than ½ in/1.5 cm from the top of the strip (diagram 2). Pin and stitch the seam and press towards the strip.

diagram 2

2 Lay the second 3½ x 6 in/9 x 15 cm strip on top of the other long edge of the triangle, right sides together, taking in the top of the first strip stitched. Pin and stitch the seam; then press as before. Using the rotary cutter, trim off the excess fabric level with the bottom of the triangle (diagram 3).

diagram 3

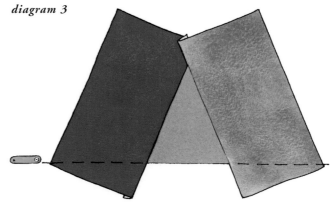

3 Take the 3½ x 9 in/9 x 23 cm strip and place over the straight edge just cut, right sides together. Pin and stitch; then press the completed block unit.

4 Using a 6½ in square rotary ruler, cut a square from the block unit, making sure that the central triangle is not cut (diagram 4). Repeat this to make a total of 48 squares. You will notice that by turning the square at random before cutting (making sure you stay within the boundaries of the block unit), you will achieve a slightly different looking block each time. This is what forms the character of the quilt.

diagram 4

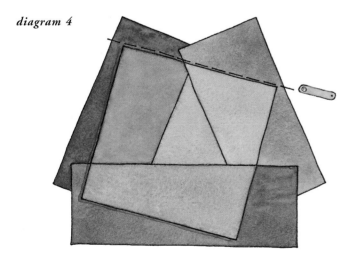

NOTE If you don't have a square ruler, draw a 6½ in/16.5 cm square from cardboard, cut a "window" in the center to help with the positioning, and use this together with a soluble marker to mark your cutting line.

5 When you have completed and pressed your 48 blocks, lay them out on the floor in eight rows of six, following the quilt assembly plan on page 70. Move around the blocks until you are happy with the layout.

6 Stitch the blocks together in horizontal rows, following the layout, taking a ¼ in/0.75 cm seam allowance. When you have completed the rows, press, and stitch the rows together, starting at the top. This completes the pieced top. Press lightly.

FINISHING

1 Measure the pieced top and cut the wadding and backing fabric at least ½ in/1.5 cm bigger on all sides.

2 Spread the backing right side down on a flat surface, then smooth the wadding and the patchwork top, right side up, on top. Fasten together with safety pins or baste in a grid.

3 If you have a twin needle sewing machine, thread with variegated thread and, following the photograph above, stitch two short lines of quilting on each block. Alternatively, stitch two parallel lines. Cut the thread long enough to stitch in afterwards (or, for speed, use the lockstitch found on some sewing machines). Then quilt "in-the-ditch" using the same variegated thread, but this is optional.

4 When the quilting is complete, stitch the binding strips together in one long strip and use to bind the edges of the quilt with a double-fold binding, mitered at the corners. Finally, add a label.

Sevens and Nines

Designed by Rosemary Wilkinson

This bright quilt is designed to be made from fat quarters in prints with a large piece of plain fabric to set off the colors. It's based on the nine-patch block but uses only seven pieces. These are arranged randomly with plain filling squares at irregular intervals. This size quilt makes a cheerful topper for a child's bed or a throw for a sunny conservatory. It can easily be made larger, either by adding more blocks or by increasing the size of each block.

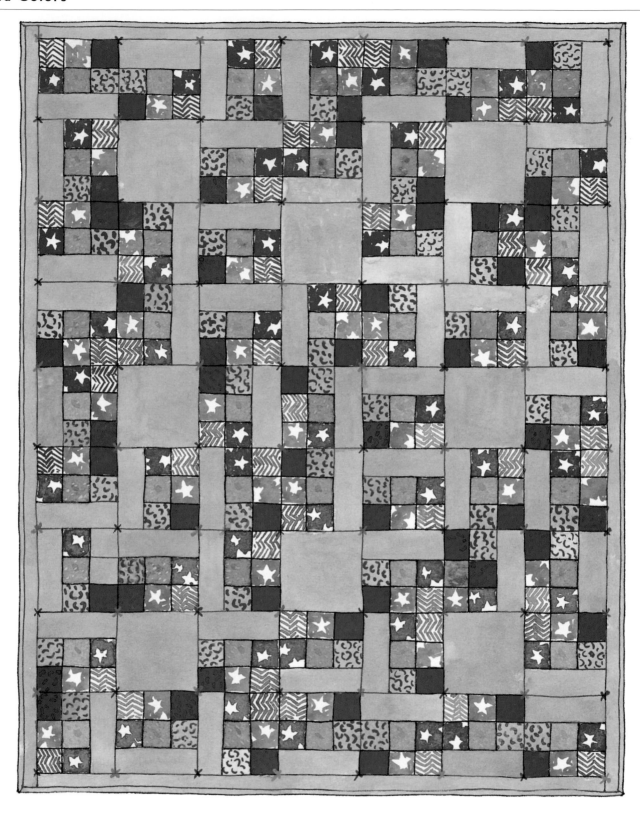

Finished size: 45 x 57 in/113 x 143 cm

MATERIALS
All fabrics in the quilt top are 45 in/115 cm wide, 100% cotton
Small squares: 6 fat quarters in red, orange and pink of small print patterns

Strips, large squares, border and binding: yellow, 1¾ yds/1.60 m
Backing: pink small print, 1¾ yds/1.60 m
Wadding: 2 oz polyester, 1¾ yds/1.60 m
Coton perlé: red and orange
Large-eyed needle

ALTERNATIVE COLOR SCHEMES

1 For a vibrant quilt use hand-dyed fabrics in the colors of the rainbow. 2 Soft and small floral prints set against calico make a very pretty, cottagey color scheme. 3 A mix of regular and irregular dotted patterns in muted colors produces a harmonious design suitable for either traditional or contemporary homes. 4 Blue and white always make a crisp and clean combination.

1

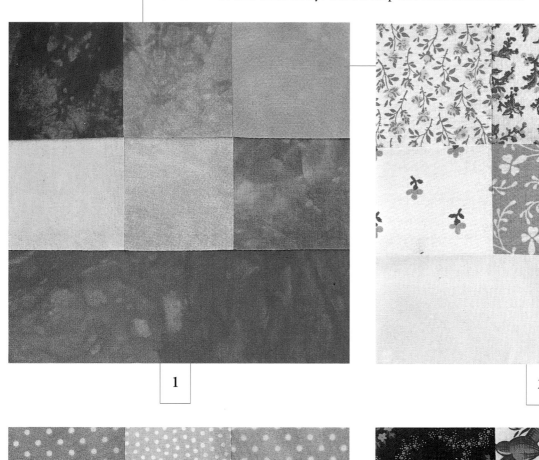

2

3

4

CUTTING

1 From each fat quarter, cut seven strips across the width, 2½ in/6.5 cm deep.

2 From the yellow fabric, cut ten strips across the width, 2½ in/6.5 cm deep; cut two strips across the width, 6½ in/16.5 cm deep; then cross-cut into 8 squares; cut five strips 2½ in/6.5 cm wide for the binding; reserve the remainder for the borders.

STITCHING

1 Place two of the fat quarter strips right sides together and stitch down one long side, taking a ¼ in/0.75 cm seam allowance.

2 Place a third strip right side down along one long edge of the unit just made and stitch as before.

3 Repeat with the remaining three fat quarter strips. Press the seams one way on the first set and the opposite way on the second.

4 Cross-cut both units into 2½ in/6.5 cm strips (diagram 1).

diagram 1

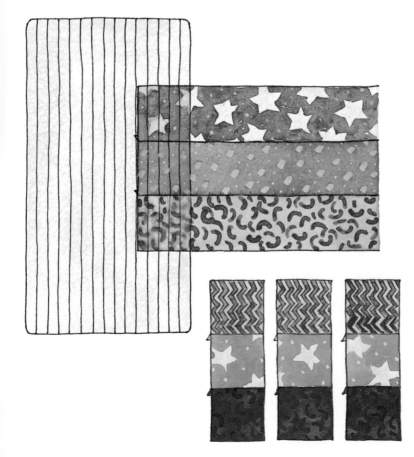

5 Chain-piece the two different short strips together in pairs. Cut, open out and press.

6 Place one of the 2½ in/6.5 cm yellow strips on top of one of the units made in step 5, aligning raw edges and stitch. Without cutting the yellow strip, add another unit underneath and stitch. Continue chain-piecing in this way until all the six-square units have been stitched to yellow strips (diagram 2).

diagram 2

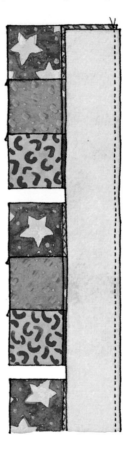

7 Trim the yellow strips level with each six-square unit, open out and press (diagram 3).

diagram 3

8 Following the quilt assembly plan on page 76, lay out the blocks interspersed with single yellow squares in your preferred arrangement, with seven blocks across and nine down.

9 Working on the two vertical rows on the lefthand side of the arrangement, chain-piece the blocks together in pairs (diagram 4). Cut, open out and press the pairs of squares; then replace in the correct positions in the quilt plan.

diagram 4

10 Repeat with vertical rows three and four; then with five and six.

11 Stitch the units together in horizontal rows, then pin and stitch the horizontal rows together, being careful to match the seams.

ADDING THE BORDERS

1 Measure the pieced top through the center from side to side; then cut two strips to this measurement and 1½ in/4 cm deep from the remaining yellow fabric. Stitch to the top and bottom of the quilt.

2 Measure the pieced top through the center from top to bottom; then cut two strips to this measurement and 1½ in/4 cm deep from the remaining yellow fabric, joined as necessary. Stitch to the sides.

FINISHING

1 Give your backing and the pieced top a good press; then spread the backing right side down on a flat surface. Smooth the wadding and the pieced top, right side up, on top. Fasten together with safety pins or baste in a grid.

2 Using coton perlé threaded into a large eye needle, tie the quilt at the intersection of each block, alternating the red and orange threads.

3 Join the binding strips into a continuous length long enough to go all around the edge of the quilt, and use to bind the quilt with a double-fold binding, mitered at the corners.

Stripes and Spots

Designed by Dorothy Wood

The use of bold stripes and spot fabric has transformed this simple design into a stunningly colorful quilt. Instead of being quilted by hand or machine, the quilt is tied together at regular intervals. Because the rectangular patchwork pieces are speed cut using a rotary cutter, the quilt top can be pieced together in a few hours. Because the design is so simple, you can easily alter the shape and size of the quilt by adding or subtracting rows or columns of blocks.

Finished size: 51½ x 80 in/131 x 204 cm

MATERIALS
All fabrics used in the quilt top are 45 in/115 cm wide 100% cotton. Backing fabric is 59 in/150 cm wide.

Yellow and white striped cotton fabric: 1¾ yds/1.50 m

Blue and white striped cotton fabric: 1¾ yds/1.50 m

Yellow and blue spot cotton fabric: 2¾ yds/2.50 m

Backing: white, 59 x 86½ in/150 x 220 cm

Wadding: 2 oz polyester, 59 x 86½ in/150 x 220 cm

White sewing thread

Large-eyed needle

Coton perlé: dark blue no. 5

ALTERNATIVE COLOR SCHEMES

1 The classic blue and white is always popular. Choose fabrics of similar weight but with different textures. 2 Because the fish motif fabric is so busy, only one plain batik fabric has been used. This creates larger areas of one fabric and pulls the design together. 3 Checks and plaids give an instant country feel. Choose a plain fabric that tones with the background color of the checks. 4 Ideal for a ballet-loving teenager, two pretty pastels have been picked out from the ballet-shoe fabric to create a harmonious, muted quilt.

1

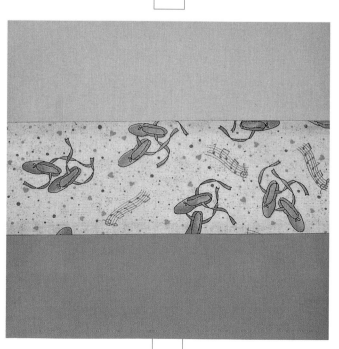

2

3

4

CUTTING

1 Cut a 2¾ yd/2.5 m strip, 12 in/30 cm wide from one long edge of the yellow and blue spot fabric and set to one side. This piece will be used later to bind the quilt.

2 Press the remaining blue spot fabric and fold in half crosswise, and then in half again. Steam-press the fabric bundle and lift onto the cutting mat. Using a rotary cutter and ruler, cut five strips across the width, 4 in/10 cm wide, then cross-cut into forty 10¾ in/27 cm rectangles.

3 Fold the striped fabrics in half crosswise once only and check that the stripes are straight on each layer. Cut ten strips across the width, 4 in/10 cm wide, then cross-cut into forty 10¾ in/27 cm rectangles.

NOTE Take extra care when folding and pressing the striped fabric to make sure that the stripes are straight on each layer before cutting.

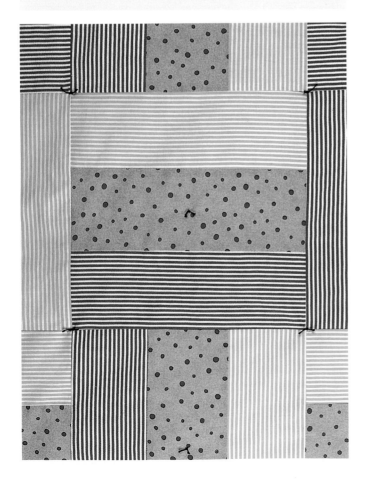

STITCHING

1 Place a yellow striped strip on top of a yellow and blue spot strip with right sides facing. Stitch the seam with a ¼ in/0.75cm seam allowance. Stitch a blue stripe strip to the other edge of the spotted strip (diagram 1). Press the seam allowances towards the striped fabric on each side. Make all forty blocks in the same way. You could chain-piece these to speed up the process.

diagram 1

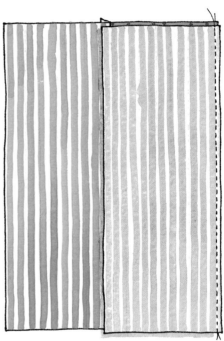

2 Check that each of the blocks is absolutely square by measuring on the cutting mat, and trim slightly if necessary. Lay five blocks in a row, alternating the stripes from horizontal to vertical. Keep the blue stripes to the lefthand side on the vertical blocks and to the bottom of the horizontal blocks throughout. Lay out all the blocks as shown in the quilt assembly plan on page 82.

3 Stitch each row of blocks together with ¼ in/0.75 cm seams. Press the seams towards the striped fabric.

4 Pin the rows together matching the seams carefully. If the seams were pressed in the right direction, the seam allowances should lie in opposite directions where they meet. Stitch the seams taking the usual seam allowance, and press all the seams towards one end of the pieced top.

FINISHING

1 Spread the backing right side down on a flat surface, then smooth the wadding and the pieced top, right side up, on top.

2 Baste around the pieced top through all the layers, ½ in/1.5 cm from the edge. Pin through all layers at each corner of the blocks.

3 To tie the quilt, thread a length of dark blue coton perlé through the large eye needle. Take a small stitch through all layers where the seams meet at the corner of the first block, and pull the thread through, leaving a 1 in/2.5 cm tail. Take a back stitch and then trim the other tail the same length (diagram 2). Pull the ends tight and tie in a reef (flat) knot. Trim the ends to ¼ in/0.75 cm.

diagram 2

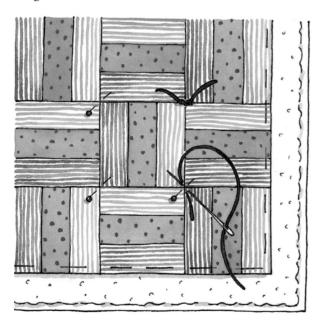

4 Stitch and tie with coton perlé at each pin. Lay the quilt out flat again. Use the quilter's ruler to find the center of each spot fabric strip and mark with a pin through all layers. Stitch and tie with perlé cotton at each pin.

5 Lay the quilt flat and smooth out carefully. Tuck a cutting mat under one edge of the quilt. Using the quilter's ruler and rotary cutter, trim the excess wadding and backing fabric ¾ in/2 cm from the edge of the quilt top. Move the cutting mat as required and cut the same measurement all the way around.

6 Cut four 2¾ yd/2.5 m, 2½ in/6.5 cm wide strips from the reserved yellow and blue spot fabric. Press the strips; then fold under and press a ¼ in/0.75 cm turning along one long side of each strip.

7 Pin the unpressed edge of one strip along the top edge of the quilt top, right sides together and aligning the raw edges. Machine stitch ¼ in/0.75 cm from the edge of the fabric though all layers. Trim level with the wadding and backing at the ends. Pin and stitch a second strip along the bottom edge of the quilt in the same way.

8 Fold the binding over to the reverse side. Slipstitch the pressed turning to the machine stitching.

9 Pin the remaining strips down the side edges, leaving ½ in/1.5 cm of fabric jutting out at either end and machine stitch (diagram 3). Turn in the excess fabric at each end; then fold the binding to the reverse. Slipstitch all the edges to complete the quilt.

diagram 3

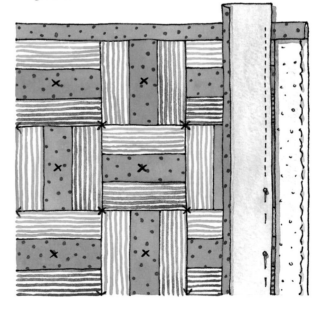

Moulin Rouge

Designed by Claire Higgott

Moulin Rouge is made with the Mary's Triangle block – a deceptively simple block which can be twisted and turned to produce dozens of different quilt designs. The relatively large pieces of the block make it perfect for showing off bold fabrics as in this stunning single bed quilt, but it also works well with more subtle colors. The blocks are quick and simple to construct using only squares and rectangles.

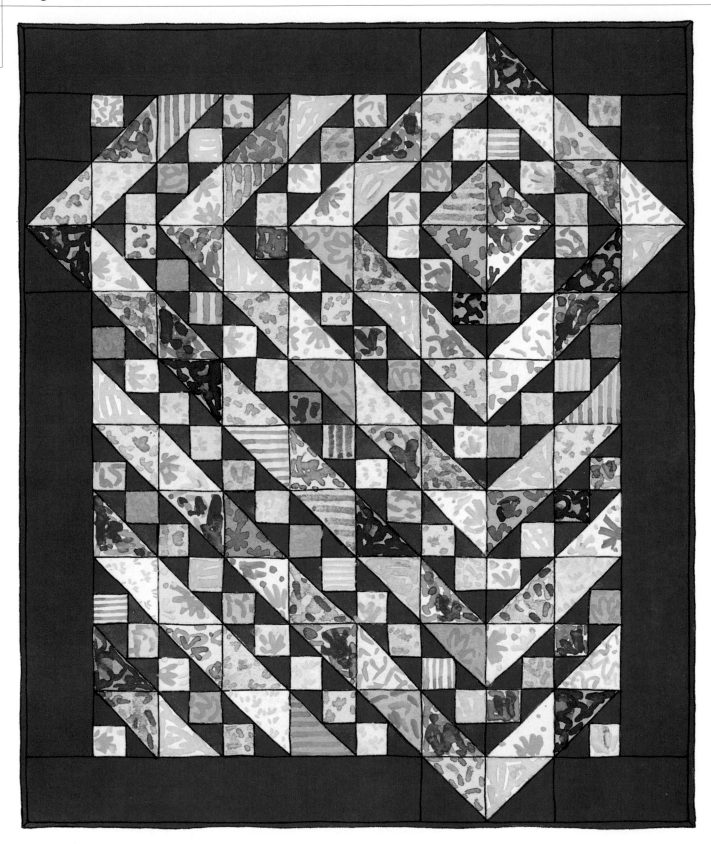

Finished size: 60 x 72 in/153 cm x 183 cm

FABRIC REQUIREMENTS
All fabrics used in the quilt top are 45 in/115 cm
wide

Blocks, border and binding: red, 2¾ yds/2.50 m
Pink and green prints: 12 fat quarters, 6 different
patterns in a mixture of these two colors
Backing: red print, 66 x 78 in/168 x 198 cm
Wadding: lightweight, 66 x 78 in/168 x 198 cm

ALTERNATIVE COLOR SCHEMES

1 Softly colored batik and marble fabrics give a gentler look to the design.
2 The pretty floral and fairy prints look crisp and summery teamed with white.
3 The large triangles are big enough to showcase bright novelty prints. Instead of using just one fabric for the rectangles, this colorway uses a variety of bright fabrics which become the small "background" triangles when the block is completed. 4 The skin prints and abstract stripe have a slightly African feel to them, and the colors really glow against the black background.

1

2

3

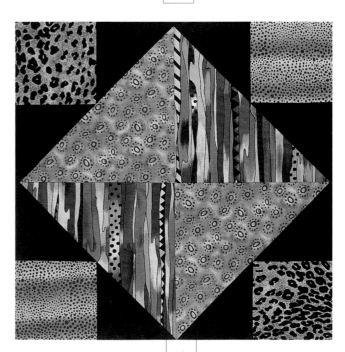

4

CUTTING

(Cut strips selvage to selvage unless otherwise
indicated.)

1 From the red fabric,
cut nine 3½ in/9 cm strips, then sub-cut into a total of
eighty 3½ x 4½ in/9 x 11.5 cm rectangles;
cut six 6½ in/16.5 cm strips; from one of these strips,
cut four 6½ x 7½ in/16.5 x 19 cm rectangles for the
border blocks;
from the next strip, cut two 6½ x 12½ in/16.5 x
31.5 cm rectangles and two 6½ in/16.5 cm squares for
the border;
cut two pieces, 6½ x 36½ in/16.5 x 91.5 cm from the
third and fourth strips for the border;
cut two pieces, 6½ x 42½ in/16.5 x 106.5 cm from the
fifth and sixth strips for the border.
The remaining red fabric will be used for the binding.

2 From each of the twelve fat quarter prints cut
seven 3½ in/9 cm squares and four 6½ x 7½ in/16.5 x
19 cm rectangles. This allows a few extra pieces. Set
aside the spare 6½ x 7½ in/16.5 x 19 cm rectangles, as
some of them will be needed for the border blocks.

STITCHING

(Use a ¼ in/0.75 cm seam allowance throughout.)
1 Stitch each of the 3½ in/9 cm printed squares to a
3½ x 4½ in/9 x 11.5 cm red rectangle. Press the seam
towards the rectangle.

2 Take two of the new units, turn one upside down
and stitch to the first (diagram 1). It doesn't matter
what color the squares are as they will end up in
different blocks.

diagram 1

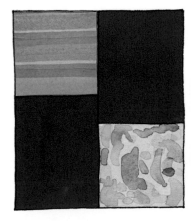

3 Snip the seam allowance in the center and press
each half of the seam towards the red rectangles.

4 On the wrong side draw stitching lines as shown
by the pencil lines (diagram 2). The lines should pass
through the inner corners of the squares.

diagram 2

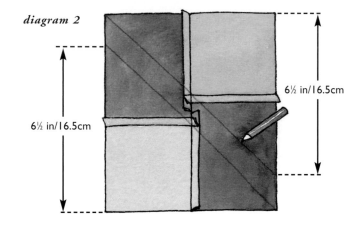

6½ in/16.5cm

6½ in/16.5cm

5 Repeat with the remaining pieced units to make a
total of forty of these pieced units. Pair one of these
units with a 6½ x 7½ in/16.5 x 19 cm print rectangle,
right sides together; this print should be different
from the small squares. Pin and stitch along both of
the marked stitching lines.

Cut between the stitched lines. The seam
allowances can be trimmed to ¼ in/0.75 cm. Open
each half out and press the seams towards the large
print triangles to make two Mary's Triangle blocks
(diagram 3).

diagram 3

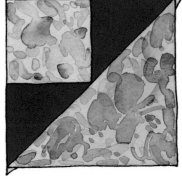

6 Repeat to make a total of eighty blocks.

7 Arrange the blocks in ten rows of eight following the quilt assembly plan on page 88.

8 Stitch the blocks in each row together, pressing the seams in opposite directions on alternate rows as you go. Then stitch the rows together. The seams should now butt together. Press. The quilt top should measure 48½ x 60½ in/121.5 x 151.5 cm at this stage.

ADDING THE BORDERS

1 To make the border blocks, choose four of the spare 6½ x 7½ in/16.5 x 19 cm print rectangles and pair each with a red one, right sides together. Draw stitching lines as shown in diagram 4.

diagram 4

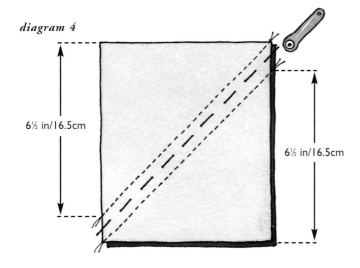

6½ in/16.5cm

6½ in/16.5cm

2 Stitch along the lines. Cut between the lines, open up and press to make eight border blocks.

3 Sort the eight border blocks into four pairs, varying the prints in each pair. Stitch the pairs of border blocks together so that the print fabrics form peaks.

4 Following the quilt assembly plan, assemble the four border sections. Stitch each border and press the seams. As you complete each border, pin a label (left, right, top, bottom) to it because they are all different!

5 Stitch the side borders onto the pieced top, making sure that the border blocks line up accurately with the blocks in the top. Press the seams toward the borders. Stitch the top and bottom borders to the quilt and press as before.

FINISHING

1 Spread the backing right side down on a flat surface, then smooth the wadding and the pieced top, right side up, on top. Fasten together with safety pins or baste in a grid.

2 Machine or hand quilt in the pattern of your choice.

NOTE
Moulin Rouge has been machine quilted on "Bertha," the long arm quilting machine at "The Bramble Patch," using an edge-to-edge design. It would also look good quilted by hand or by machine "in-the-ditch" to emphasize the diagonal lines.

3 From the remaining red fabric, cut seven 2 in/5 cm strips, selvage to selvage. Trim off the selvages; then join the strips of binding with 45 degree seams. Trim off the excess fabric; then press the seams open. The angled seam helps to spread the bulk of the join.

4 Fold the binding in half along the length and use to bind the quilt with a double-fold binding mitered at the corners. Don't forget to add a label to your quilt!

All Fenced In

Designed by Sarah Wellfair

After spending a few days helping my son Nick to make his first quilt using the rail fence pattern, I decided to try to take the traditional block and make it more interesting. First I put it on point; then fenced it in with triangles and finally sashed it together. The resulting lap quilt was very quick and easy to make using quick piecing and rotary equipment.

Finished size: 58 x 58 in/147 x 147 cm

MATERIALS
All fabrics used in the quilt top are 45 in/115 cm
wide, 100% cotton
Square blocks: orange, 20 in/55 cm; yellow,
20 in/55 cm

Triangles and sashing squares: blue, 40 in/1.10 m
Sashing strips: gold, 42 in/1.10 m
Binding: orange, 20 in/50 cm
Backing: blue, 3¼ yds/3 m
Wadding: 2 oz polyester, 60 x 60 in/152 x 152 cm
Threads: to match fabrics for quilting

ALTERNATIVE COLOR SCHEMES

1 The small floral prints merge together to give the impression of one flowery fabric. 2 The chicken novelty print makes this into a fun quilt for a child. 3 Pretty pinks and creams would suit a country cottage bedroom. 4 A harmonious matching of mauve and purple checks and floral prints produces an elegant colorway.

1

2

3

4

CUTTING

1 From the orange fabric, cut 8 strips 2½ in/6.5 cm deep across the full width of fabric.

2 From the yellow fabric, cut 8 strips 2½ in/6.5 cm deep across the full width of fabric.

3 From the blue fabric for the triangles and sashing squares, cut 16 squares 9¼ x 9¼ in/ 23.5 x 23.5 cm and cross-cut each one into four quarter-square triangles; cut 25 squares, 3 x 3 in/7.5 x 7.5 cm.

STITCHING

1 Take one orange and one yellow strip and place right sides together; then stitch together down one long side, taking a ¼ in/0.75 cm seam allowance. Do the same to the remaining seven orange and seven yellow strips.

2 Take two of the pairs and place right sides together with an orange strip on top of a yellow one. Stitch together down one long side, taking the usual seam allowance, so that you have four strips of alternate colors. Repeat with the remaining strips. You should now have four pieces with four strips in each. Press the seams towards the darker fabric. These strips should now measure approximately 8½ in/21.5 cm across.

3 Using a rotary cutter and ruler, cross-cut the strips into 8½ in/21.5 cm squares. This should make 20 squares. You will need 16 of these for your quilt.

4 Stitch one of the quarter square blue triangles to the top and bottom of each orange and yellow square (diagram 1). Do the same on the other two sides. Press the seams towards the blue triangles.

diagram 1

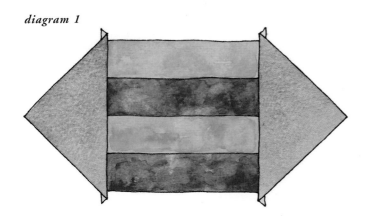

5 Arrange these squares in four rows, four across, following the quilt assembly plan on page 94.

6 Measure across the middle of each square and take an average measurement. Cut 40 sashing strips from the gold fabric to this length and 3 in/7.5 cm wide.

7 Stitch one sashing strip to the top of each square; then stitch the squares together in vertical rows.

8 Stitch one sashing strip to the end of each row (diagram 2). You should now have four rows of four blocks with sashing in between.

diagram 2   *diagram 3*

9 Take the rest of the sashing strips and stitch one small blue square to the end of each strip; then stitch the strips together into five lengths. Finally, take the five remaining small blue squares and stitch one to the end of each length (diagram 3). Press all the seams towards the gold sashing.

10 Stitch the sashing strips to the left side of each of the four rows of blocks; then stitch the rows together. Stitch the last sashing strip to the righthand edge of the pieced top. Press the top for the last time and cut off any unwanted threads.

FINISHING

1 Measure the pieced top through the center from side to side, and cut and join the backing fabric to this size, plus 2 in/5 cm on all sides.

2 Spread the backing right side down on a flat surface, then smooth the wadding and the pieced top, right side up, on top. Fasten together with safety pins or baste in a grid.

3 Quilt as desired. I used a three step zig-zag in the sashings and free quilted in the blocks.

4 Trim the excess backing and wadding level with the pieced top.

5 Cut the binding fabric across the width into strips 3 in/7.5 cm deep and stitch across the short sides, right sides together, to form one long length of binding. Fold in half, wrong sides together along the length, and press.

6 Measure the quilt through the center from side to side and cut two strips of binding to this length. Pin one of these to the top of the quilt, matching raw edges, and stitch, taking a ¼ in/0.75 cm seam allowance. Repeat at the bottom of the quilt.

7 Turn each binding strip to the back of the quilt and slip stitch to the quilt covering the stitching line.

8 Measure the quilt through the center from top to bottom and cut bindings to this length, plus 1½ in/4 cm. Pin one of these binding strips to the left-hand side of the quilt, overlapping by ¾ in/2 cm at each end. Stitch taking the usual seam allowance.

9 Fold in the short ends, turn the binding strip to the back and slipstitch down as before (diagram 4). Repeat to bind the righthand side of the quilt.

diagram 4

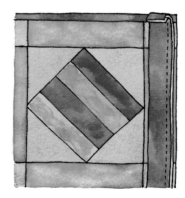

10 Your quilt is now ready to be signed and dated.

Treasures Cot Quilt

Designed by Gail Smith

The treasures cot quilt was so called because of the bright fabrics used and also the treasured baby that it might be made for. Babies grow, however, and this simple block-by-block quilt grows very quickly, too, so that it could be easily made larger than the example shown here, which is made up of twelve blocks. It could also be made from scraps or a fat quarter collection.

Finished size: 33 x 43 in/79.5 x 103.5 cm

MATERIALS
All fabrics used in the quilt top are 45 in/115 cm wide, 100% cotton

NOTE   If the fabric you've chosen for the center squares and the outer border is a "busy" fabric; then I would suggest a calmer fabric for their borders.

Four-patch center squares and outer border: a long quarter (¼ yd or 25 cm) across the bolt of at least seven different bright fabrics.

Border around each four patch-center: assuming you will use each fabric for two blocks, 6 in/15 cm strips cut across the bolt of six toning or contrasting fabrics

Binding: 6 in/15 cm of chosen fabric, cut across the bolt

Backing: butterfly print cotton or sheeting, 36 x 45 in/91 x 115 cm

Wadding: 2 oz polyester or a cotton alternative, 36 x 45 in/91 x 115 cm

Variegated machine thread: either rayon or cotton

ALTERNATIVE COLOR SCHEMES

The Treasures Cot Quilt design will lend itself to lots of different fabrics. Brights, plains or traditional patterns will sit comfortably together as shown in the four different colorways below. Why not try soft fleece on the back as an alternative to the wadding and cotton backing?

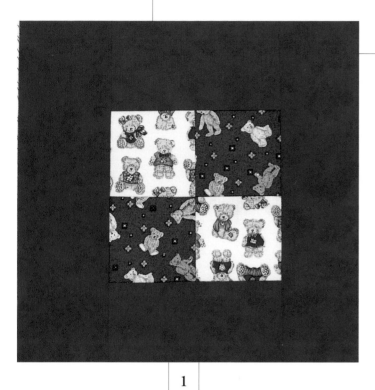

1

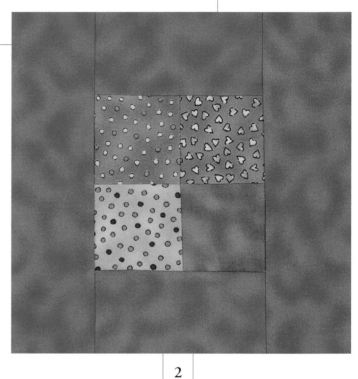

2

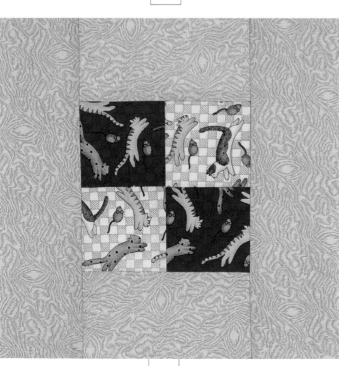

3

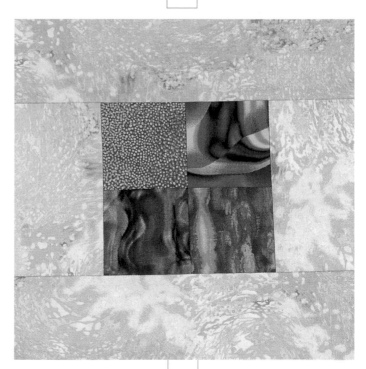

4

CUTTING

1 From each of the fabrics chosen for the center squares of the blocks and the outer border, cut one 3 in/7.5 cm strip. Cross-cut the strips into 3 in/7.5 cm squares. Put these to one side.

2 From each of the six fabrics that border the four-patch centers, cut one 3 in/7.5 cm strip across the width.

3 Cut the binding fabric into 1½ in/4 cm strips.

4 Do not cut the backing until you have finished stitching.

STITCHING

1 Jumble the squares in a carrier bag and select, at random, two squares at a time to stitch together, each with ¼ in/0.75 cm seam allowance. Using the chain-piecing method, stitch 24 pairs of squares together. (I usually peek to make sure that no two are the same!) Reserve the rest of the squares until later. When you have your 24 pairs, cut to separate, open out and press the seams to one side.

2 Next, again choosing at random, stitch two sets of pairs together, 12 times, giving 12 mini four-patch blocks (diagram 1). Press all the seams to one side. (Keep the remaining squares for the outer border.)

diagram 1

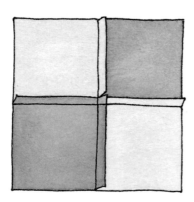

3 To add borders to each four-patch block, take a 3 x 45 in/7.5 x 115 cm strip of your chosen fabric and place it on top of a four-patch block, aligning raw edges and right sides together. Stitch, then trim level with the edge of the four-patch block (diagram 2).

diagram 2

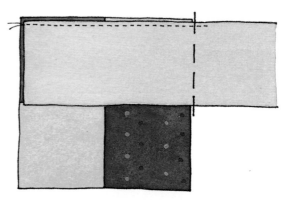

4 Repeat to add another strip to the bottom of the block (diagram 3). Press the seams towards the darker fabric.

diagram 3

NOTE To speed up this process, you could stitch all the top border pieces first; then all the bottom pieces.

5 Repeat to add the border strip to the sides of the blocks (diagram 4). Press.

diagram 4

6 Lay the completed blocks on the floor, all the same way up (short border to the top), following the quilt assembly plan on page 100. Try different layouts until you are happy with this, and try not to have two blocks the same or similar next to each other.

7 Stitch three blocks together in a strip. Repeat to make four strips. Press.

8 Working down from the top, stitch the first strip to the second; then add the third and fourth, as in your layout. When complete, press lightly.

ADDING THE BORDERS

1 Taking the 3 in/7.5 cm squares left over from the first stage, at random, stitch enough of these together to make two strips long enough for the sides and two for the top and bottom borders. This should be 18 squares for the sides and 12 for the top and bottom of the pieced top. Chain-piece in pairs if you wish to speed up the process. Press.

2 Stitch a border strip to the top and bottom of the quilt; then to each side. You have now completed your quilt top.

FINISHING

1 Measure the completed quilt top, and cut wadding and backing fabric at least ½ in/1.5 cm bigger on all sides.

2 Spread the backing right side down on a flat surface, then smooth the wadding and the pieced top, right side up, on top. Fasten together with safety pins or baste in a grid.

3 Using a walking foot and the decorative stitches on your sewing machine, ideally a scallop or wave pattern, quilt in lines down and across the quilt, as desired.

4 Join the binding strips into one length, long enough to go all around the quilt, and use to bind the quilt with a single-fold binding, mitered at the corners.

Country Coverlet

Designed by Gill Turley

A cheerful quilt made from odd pieces of checked and striped cottons and edged with a crisp border of prairie points. The felt coin dots plus the borders of bright triangles pick out the colors from the checks used in the center section. This simple quilt looks fantastic as a top quilt over a plain cream counterpane or sheet. Alternatively, it would make a great throw over the back of a sofa. It's hand quilted with coton à broder thread, but for speed the quilting could be done by machine. Ties secure the quilt layers in the center section, and these are stitched through the decorative coin dots.

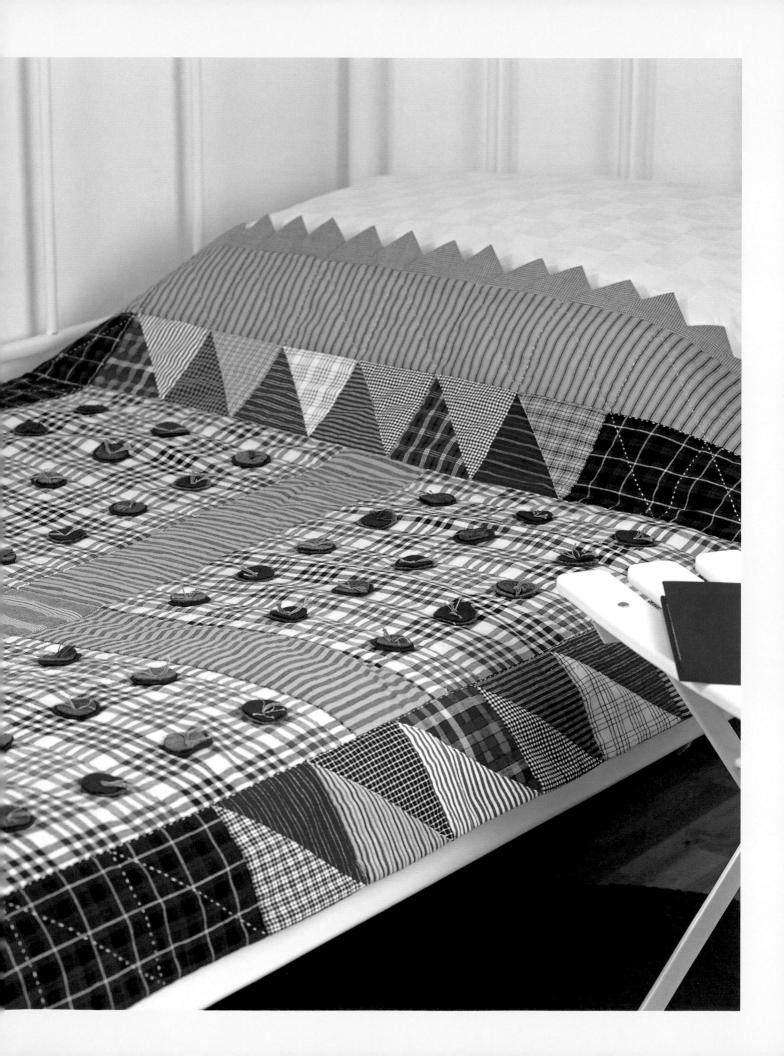

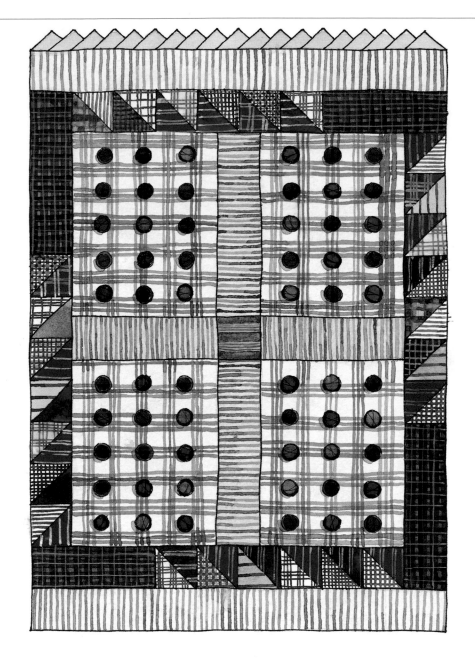

Finished size: 56 x 40 in/145 x 100 cm (including the prairie points edging)

MATERIALS

Large check fabric for center rectangles: four pieces, each measuring 18½ x 14½ in/46.5 x 36.5 cm (pieces **1**, **2**, **3** and **4**)

Striped fabric for center strips, top and bottom borders: two 18½ x 4½ in/46.5 x 11.5 cm (pieces **a** and **b**); two co-ordinating pieces 14½ x 4½ in/36.5 x 11.5 cm (pieces **c** and **d**);

For center square: one piece 4½ x 4½ in/11.5 x 11.5 cm (piece **e**)

Border triangles: bright striped and checked cottons in assorted colors:

thirteen light/medium squares, 5 x 5 in/13 x 13 cm

thirteen dark squares, 5 x 5 in/13 x 13 cm

Border strips: darker checked fabric:
two long strips, 16½ x 4½ in/41.5 x 11.5 cm
two short strips, 12½ x 4½ in/31.5 x 11.5 cm

Striped fabric for top and bottom outer borders:
two pieces, each 40½ x 4½ in/101.5 x 11.5 cm

Prairie points edging: lightweight fabric, one strip, 40 x 8 in/100 x 20 cm

Felt for coin dots: washable felt in assorted colors: four pieces 12 x 12 in/30 x 30 cm

Backing: small check, 60 x 44 in/150 x 110 cm

Wadding: cotton, 60 x 44 in/155 x 110 cm

Thread for quilting and ties: coton à broder no. 16 or similar

Large quilting hoop (optional)

Large-eyed needle

ALTERNATIVE COLOR SCHEMES

1 Earth colors of brown, ochre, rust and gold blend together well and create a warm look. Bright red coin dots set off the flowery print. 2 Soft checks, stripes and dots enhance the ladybird fabric chosen for the center section. Triangles in red and green, plus a strip of flame red, add warmth. 3 Framed by strips of jewel colored fabric, the pink and cream flower trellis makes an interesting choice for the center. The rich pink triangles placed next to the soft cream ones add strength. 4 Fresh blue, green and white fabrics give a crisp look. These are mainly stripes and checks, but small prints work well in the triangles.

1

2

3

4

STITCHING

1 To make the central section, stitch pieces **1** and **2** to center strip **a** and pieces **3** and **4** to strip **b**. Press the seams towards the strips. Stitch center strips **c** and **d** to center square **e**, pressing the seams away from the square. Next join the top section to the bottom section with the center strip in the middle. Press these seams away from the center strip (diagram 1).

diagram 1

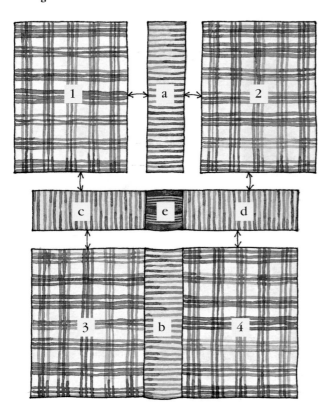

2 To make the triangle units for the borders, place the thirteen dark and thirteen light/medium squares right sides together, pairing light/medium squares with dark squares. Draw a pencil line diagonally from corner to corner; then stitch on each side of the diagonal line ¼ in/0.75 cm away from pencil marking (diagram 2). For speed these units can be chain-pieced.

diagram 2

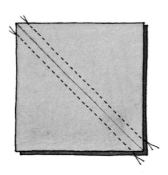

3 When the stitching stage has been completed, snip the squares apart; then cut along the pencil lines. Press these units open, making sure that the seams are pressed towards the darker fabric. Trim the pieced units to the correct size, 4½ x 4½ in/11.5 x 11.5 cm.

ADDING THE BORDERS

1 For the top and bottom borders, join together six triangle units and press the seams toward the dark fabric. Add the short border strips of darker checked fabric to complete. Press the seams towards the strips (diagram 3).

diagram 3

2 For each of the side borders, join together seven triangle units and press seams as before. To each side border now add a long border strip of darker checked fabric.

3 Pin one of the side borders to the lefthand edge of the quilt with the triangle section at the bottom. Begin stitching in the strip section just above the first triangle, leaving most of the strip section of the border free. Stitch all the way down to the bottom edge. Press the seams towards the center of the quilt.

4 Pin the bottom border to the bottom edge of the quilt, and this time stitch the full length of the border. Press seams as before.

5 Pin and stitch the righthand side border and the top border in the same way.

6 Finally, stitch down the unsewn section of the lefthand side border and press seams.

7 Stitch the striped fabric top and bottom outer borders in place, and press the seams away from the pieced borders.

MAKING THE PRAIRIE POINTS

1 This stage is best completed at the ironing board. Have your scissors handy. To make the prairie points, place the lightweight fabric on the ironing board and press it in half lengthwise; then open it out again. Starting at the bottom right hand corner make a 45-degree fold so that the raw, side edge of the fabric meets the center line; then press. Make a cut alongside the edge of the piece you have just folded. Only cut as far as the center line (diagram 4a).

diagram 4a

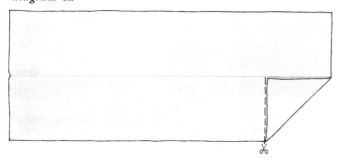

2 Continue in the same way until all the first stage folds on the lower half have been completed.

3 To complete the second stage, make a second fold so that the raw edges of each triangle meet the center line; then press (diagram 4b).

diagram 4b

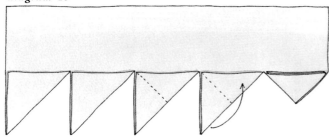

4 To make the points on the opposite edge you will need to offset the triangles. Turn the strip so that the unfolded edge is now nearest to you. Begin by trimming away the first and last 2 in/5 cm of this section; then make the folds and cuts as before (diagram 4c).

diagram 4c

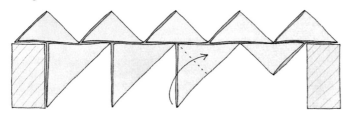

5 Next fold along the center line and slot the triangles, one inside the other. Press well and run a line of machine stitching close to the edge of the long (center) fold to prevent the prairie points (triangles) from slipping out of place (diagram 4d).

diagram 4d

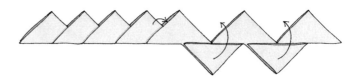

6 Position the strip of prairie points along the top edge of the quilt, placing the long fold edge of the strip on the top edge of the right side of the quilt. The points should be pointing towards the quilt. Baste the strip in place. Stitch through all layers.

FINISHING

1 Place the backing fabric on a flat surface, right side up, and use masking tape or pins to hold it in place. Carefully position the quilt top, wrong side up, on top of the backing. Make sure all layers are smooth and pin the edges together, leaving the edge with prairie points open. Stitch the three pinned edges together.

NOTE Be careful not to stitch across the points of the pieced triangles, as this will spoil the look of the finished quilt.

2 When the stitching has been completed and with the quilt still inside out, place it on the wadding, working on a flat surface as before.

3 Pin carefully and stitch through all three layers using the initial stitching line as a guide. The top edge is still unstitched at this stage. Trim away any excess wadding and backing fabric and turn the quilt through to the right side.

NOTE Make sure that the corners are fully pushed out, and gently roll the edges between the thumb and first finger so that you achieve a firm edge. At this stage it is worth basting around the stitched edges to hold the layers in position. Although the sides of the quilt have been stitched together, you will need to baste or safety pin the layers to keep them from moving during the quilting stage. The top edge remains open until the quilting has been completed.

4 Begin by quilting a few lines across the large rectangles, using the check as a guide. Quilt around each rectangle, quilting "in-the-ditch." Continue quilting around the edge of the triangles; then echo these triangle shapes on the solid sections of the borders. Treat the top and bottom borders in the same way, but don't quilt the top border.

5 To make the coin dots, draw around a large and a medium sized spool to make rough circles on the felt pieces. You will need a total of 60 large and 60 small coin dots of mixed colors.

6 Place a small circle on a large one, varying the colors within each section. Working on one center section at a time, position the coins dots in a regular pattern on the center rectangles, and pin them in place. It helps to place the work in a large quilting hoop if you have one.

7 Thread a large needle with a length of coton à broder. Take the needle through the center of the coin dot from the front of the work to the back; then bring it back through to the front, coming up through the coin dot again. Tie the ends in a reef knot and snip the threads, leaving ends of approximately ½ in/1.5 cm. Continue in the same way until all four center sections have been completed.

8 On the back of the quilt, turn in the unfinished edge, baste first, and then slip stitch in place. The turned-in edge should just cover the stitching line of the prairie points, and these points should now be standing proud at the top edge of the quilt.

9 To complete, finish the remaining quilting on the top border.

HISTORICAL NOTE

Coin dots were popular in Victorian times and also in later years. They were often sewn edge-to-edge and used to make "penny rugs," the name penny coming from the old, large penny coins used as templates. The "coins" could also be placed edge-to-edge and over-sewn onto a backing fabric to provide a warm bed cover. If felt was not available, coin dots were made from old clothing, especially woolen items that had been well washed and felted with use.

INDEX